Moonlight Over the Canal

Moonlight Over the Canal

Stories from a Girl's Life in Historical Morris County, New Jersey

Ruth Wilma Shults

Mill City Press, Inc.

Moonlight Over the Canal
Stories from a Girl's Life in Historical Morris County, New Jersey

Mill City Press, Inc.
212 N. 3rd Avenue, Suite 471
Minneapolis, MN 55401
www.MillCityPress.net

ISBN - 13: 978-1-934248-08-9
ISBN - 10: 1-934248-08-8

Printed in the United States of America

In memory of
Sarah Virginia (Jennie) Van Duyne
Bill and Marie Reif, my parents
and
Dick and Jean Chipman

We are only temporary custodians of whatever we have stored in our brain. It's not going to stay there all the time. You have to pass it on so somebody else can pick it up and go on.

—Bernhardt Crystal

Contents

Foreword

Our little town changed for me after reading *Moonlight Over the Canal*. Common local places seemed to take on a more intimate aspect. Part auto-biography, part history, Ruth Wilma Shults's account of her childhood lends a rich and fascinating dimension to houses, places, local personalities, and even the long gone Morris Canal featured in the title of her work.

Historic preservation is a priority in the area of Morris County, New Jersey, where the author spent her youth. Shults relates how her temporary home—the eighteenth-century Martin J. Van Duyne House—survived in the path of a proposed interstate highway. More remarkable for our town is the survival of the other fourteen extant Dutch-American stone farmhouses, which have been here more than two hundred years. Montville Township has the highest concentration of such intact early dwellings in the Garden State.

Considered important points in New Jersey's Crossroads of the American Revolution National Heritage Area, Montville Township and Boonton are proud of their exceptional heritage. Their dilemma was determining how to preserve local historical sites. Like many other governing bodies faced with rapid development pressures, the Montville Township Committee sought to buttress local land use regulation to protect its cultural resources. Fortunately, the New Jersey Legislature cooperated by amending the state's municipal land use code to enable townships to afford that protection.

Montville's first step was to survey and identify historic sites in town. Then it created a historic preservation element in its master plan, including an ordinance and a historic preservation review commission. More than one hundred buildings and sites were identified. Shults vividly describes many of them.

All of this means the features covered in Shults's childhood memories are preserved in reality as well as on these pages.

S. David Phraner
Canal Society of New Jersey

Introduction

Some might say that I was born at the wrong time. I directly experienced the devastation of my father's financial loss during the Great Depression and remotely felt the impact of the horrors of World War II. But the pastoral life I lived for nineteen years on two pieces of property in Morris County, New Jersey, shielded and nourished me during my childhood and adolescence. I lived for nine years on the land and in the Dutch-American stone farmhouse of Martin J. Van Duyne in Montville—a place my parents rented from Sarah Virginia (Jennie) Van Duyne. This was followed by ten years living on land my parents developed and on which my father built his last house—property that was originally part of the Miller-Kingsland tract in Boonton.

This lush, small lake-dotted area of northern New Jersey was a living schoolroom in which I dreamed of my future life and observed how my parents dealt with their unplanned circumstances. Farm life was hard on my parents, but for me it was a time of adventure. In order to provide food for the family during the Depression my parents raised goats and chickens and plowed a very large vegetable garden, which became the source of an extensive summertime canning operation. My mother remarked one dinnertime that all that was on the table, with the exception of coffee and spices, came from their labors.

I learned the significance of community from my experience living on the farm. Neighbors showed my parents how to buy, raise, and slaughter goats and chickens and how to can food on a large scale. In turn, mother prepared a wholesome breakfast for the traveling men who walked the highway in front of the old house. These men would receive three sunny-side-up eggs, homemade sausage, fried potatoes, bread, and as many cups of coffee as they wanted. I became the willing waitress. Such lessons of giving back to the community have stayed with me throughout my life.

When we moved to Boonton I entered Boonton High School. There, as a young lady, I developed the skills to make my childhood dreams come true.

Majoring in business classes, receiving a civics award in high school, and graduating from Barbizon Modeling School, I attained the confidence to face the future. I moved from the home of a farming community to one of prosperous landowners and successful New York businessmen. Although I retained my friends who played in the Wood's family barn and skated on the old Morris Canal, my new friends lived in town and their fathers were merchants.

This was the period when the war ended successfully, and the nation felt buoyant with its new optimism and abundant opportunities. My father re-established his construction business, and my mother no longer had to work the farm. When at age eighteen I boarded the Delaware, Lackawanna, and Western Railroad and traveled to New York City to work, I became a manifestation of all that post-World War II represented. I was a young lady on the move. Such were the times. Such were the splendors and challenges of my childhood.

My life journey has taken me through different cities. In my fond memories of all the places I have lived, the most beautiful are from the years in the Martin J. Van Duyne Dutch-American stone farmhouse in Montville, New Jersey, and on the Miller-Kingsland property in Boonton, New Jersey.

Part One

The Martin J. Van Duyne Dutch-American Stone Farmhouse, Montville, New Jersey

1935 to 1944

On December 23, 1930, Marie Reif, my mother, gave birth to a seven-pound, four-ounce baby girl. She and my dad, George Adam (Bill) Reif, named their only child Ruth Wilma. Mother told me I was named Ruth because they liked a professional dancer by the same name. Wilma came from my godparents' only daughter. After Mother's stay in the hospital, my parents brought me home to Lincoln Park, nestled in the northern New Jersey lake area. Lincoln Park was, and still is, a commuter town from where white-collar and professional people took the Delaware, Lackawanna, and Western (DL&W) Railroad to work in New York City. Dad did not commute to the city but had a successful construction company in Lincoln Park. My parents brought me home to one of the houses he built on Longview Drive. A year later, we moved into the ground floor of a larger three-story, three-unit, brick apartment building he built on Main Street.

Two years after the move, the bank in which Dad had his money failed. This forced him into bankruptcy, and we ultimately lost our beautiful home to his creditors. In the spring of 1935, when I was four and a half, my father moved us to a Dutch-American stone farmhouse in Montville, a small rural community six miles northwest of Lincoln Park. Although this house was a major downgrade from where we had lived, the rent was cheap, and the land provided the means to raise animals and grow the vegetables needed to feed the family.The house was the Martin J. Van Duyne house, built in 1789—eight years after the American Revolution. The Van Duyne house was one of many Dutch-American stone farmhouses dotting the hills and valleys of this part of Morris County. This particular property may have been the only house available for my parents to rent considering their means.

I could not have predicted the positive impact this turn of fate would have on my future development. I doubt if my parents shared my feelings of good fortune.

*   *   *   *

When Dad turned his 1926 Chevrolet truck onto the property over a rocky tree-lined driveway, I had my first look at my new home, that we would be sharing with the last owner, Sarah Virginia (Jennie) Van Duyne. At that moment, the glance Mother gave Dad made me anxious. What I saw from the front seat of our truck, however, was very pleasant, and I soon forgot their unspoken message. To the left was our new house with its white-framed, shuttered windows and two white doors. In front was a square wood box that covered a well. Dad pointed out three very large oak trees shading the house and the lawn. White lilies of the valley grew in the shaded areas next to the basement door. At the side of the house was a large maple tree on which I envisioned a swing. On the opposite side of the driveway was a row of large maple and oak trees. Beyond the trees was a large open field that Mother said would become our vegetable garden, which I could help plant, if I wanted to.

The driveway ended in front of a large, weather-beaten, dilapidated barn with shingles and siding missing. Lumber, partially hidden by weeds, became visible as we drove closer. Some of the weeds had flowers, but mostly they were green. The fields surrounding the house and barn were overrun with small bushy plants. These surroundings did not look anything like the well-manicured yard of the brick house where I had lived. It had had a sidewalk on which I could ride my tricycle. I thought the barn and open fields might be a satisfactory tradeoff, though.

As soon as Dad parked the truck, I jumped out and started to run to the well, but he stopped me. Instead he and mother led me up the Morris Canal embankment to show me the canal, which had ceased to operate in 1924. I would soon find out that this was one of their concerns in renting the property. We sat on the towpath not only to enjoy the beauty of what remained of the old waterway, but also for them to impress upon me the possible dangers the canal presented. They told me stories of young children who drowned in the canal because they were not careful. Summer accidents were often caused by falling into the water when the rain-soaked embankment gave way. In the winter the danger was skating on thin ice. I heard all this, but the canal became enchanted as the sun filtered through the trees that outlined the canal banks. I became lost in its beauty, and my parents' words became secondary.

We walked back down the embankment, and when I saw the well I ran to it. The top had a stone base that supported a wooden rim, and on top of that was a wood cover. Adjacent to the well cover were two poles. Dad walked to my side to tell me that the poles were called well sweeps and to explain the principles of drawing water from a well. He told me I could draw water only when an adult was with me.

Dad moved a large stone for me to stand on so I could reach over the top of the wooden rim. Then he removed the cover. He pulled the vertical pole of the well sweep towards me, and I took hold of it. Hand over hand we lowered the pail into the stone-lined, spring-fed well until it touched the water. When I heard the splash, I squealed with delight. Dad pushed the pail into the water; when it was full, the vertical pole dropped farther into the well. He reached over to pull the pole back to me so I could retrieve the pail, but it did not budge. We laughed. Dad then put his hands over mine, and together we pulled up the pail filled with fresh water.

I used a tin cup to dip water from the pail. Mother, Dad, and I drank from the water I drew. How good it tasted. It was cold, and the metal cup against my lips made the water taste even colder. That day I started a nine-year love affair with my new home.

At the house, Mother opened the top half of the Dutch door. I was just tall enough to see over it. She explained that the split door was used to keep cattle out of the house. We later used the half-door to keep the farm cats from proudly depositing half-chewed garden snakes in front of the kitchen sink. The floor in this room was dirt, and before we could move in Dad had to lay a cement floor and convert the storage room into a kitchen. The doorframe was low, and the ceiling in this room was also low. Later when my tall cousins visited, they had to stoop down to enter the house, and once inside they had to stand between the beams in the ceiling.

The kitchen would have a combination coal and wood stove, an icebox, a hand pump at the wash sink, and a Maytag wringer clothes-washing machine. At one end was a water closet; there was no room for a standard bathroom.

To the left and up two stairs was a very large room that would be used as a combination dining-living room. It had high ceilings. The fireplace, typical of the homes of that era, was large enough for me to stand in. Dad would cement over the flue and connect a coal-wood burning stove to provide our heat. The built-in cabinet next to the fireplace would hold my toys.

Over the room that would be the kitchen were two small rooms, which would become our bedrooms. Mine was the smallest. It had a little window with a deep windowsill. From there I could see the barn and the wooded area behind the house. During the hot summer, I would reposition my bed so I could put my pillow on the windowsill and catch a breeze to cool me. My room would be furnished with my twin bed, a dresser, and a small wood chair.

After exploring the well and the house, the barn became my next focus. Although I was told not to enter it without an adult, the positioning of the open doors beckoned me. They were resting against the barn and were partly off their hinges, giving the image of someone very drunk. From the threshold of the open doors, I peeked inside to see a floor covered with rusted things that I had never seen before. Some planks were missing, and there was dirt below them. I looked up into the rafters and saw sunlight streaming into the open space in the center of the barn. But there was an unpleasant smell all around me. I did not know where the smell came from—decaying animals or rotting wood—but I was not sure how far inside I wanted to venture. I took a few steps and then stopped when my legs would not go farther. They were trembling, and I wanted to pee. I moved out of the doorway, squatted, and relieved myself.

My active imagination envisioned finding a dead body, and the thought started my heart pounding. When I made another move forward, a flock of birds took flight from parts unknown, and I ran screaming for dear life. Mother came running from the house, following my screams not knowing in what condition she would find her daughter. When she caught me running from the barn, she swatted the back of my head and told me never to go in there again.

Dad knew that admonishment would not last. Besides, we were living on a farm where such adventures were part of life. Since he was a carpenter, he gave the barn a thorough inspection, made it as childproof as he could, and told me what parts to avoid.

As we explored the property, I was filled with expectations of new adventures. But when I moved closer to my mother, I felt her apprehension and disappointment. We had just moved from a beautiful house with all the modern conveniences, and I sensed her sadness. Her life had changed. My parents came from good stock and knew what they needed to do for survival. Mother could have gone into a depression, but she rolled up her sleeves and worked hard. She must have drawn some of that strength from her mother—a remarkable woman according to the stories I had been told. I was born a year after Grandmother died.

After Dad prepared half of the house for our living quarters as best he could, Mother put her decorating skills to work. Her first challenge was the living room walls. Throughout the house, the walls were as thick as the stones that formed them. On the inside of the house, the stone walls were plastered to give them a smooth surface. She decided to cover them with brightly patterned wallpaper, but later the winter dampness penetrated the stones, and the wallpaper buckled. Mother removed the wallpaper that buckled, painted over the plastered walls, and repapered those sections. I thought the buckled paper was fun to push on.

The windows were flush with the outside of the house, creating windowsills inside that were about two feet deep since the outer walls were that thick. For these, Mother made cushions to sit on and to add color to the room. Many of the small glass panes in the double-hung windows (six above and six below) consisted of old glass with imperfections that caused distorted images not unlike those in a haunted house at a carnival. I enjoyed watching the misshapen images created by passing cars.

The floor planks were warped—their edges turned upwards. In some places the grout between them was missing. In these spots, we could see into the basement. Dad filled in the missing grout but could do nothing with the warped boards. We placed furniture where it wouldn't wobble.

After a few weeks of hard work, Dad was satisfied that our half of the Van Duyne house was livable, so we moved in. He used his truck to make several trips and had friends and neighbors helping him. I remember very little of the move. It seemed as though one minute I lived in the suburbs and the next I lived on a farm. Although I cried when we moved, deep down I knew the farm would be fun.

*   *   *   *

On May 3, 1771, James Van Duyne (1732-1811) purchased sixty acres from Adam Demout (Demouth). This was originally part of a land grant from King George III as ownership of land was being transferred from the Indians to the white settlers. The first parcel was 52.28 acres on which the Martin J. Van Duyne house stands today. The second parcel of 7.72 acres lay along the east side of Valhalla Road from Main Road to the brook and probably contained the tanyard.[1] Over the next forty years, James bought additional land adjacent to his original purchase.

Martin J. Van Duyne[2] was born August 25, 1763 and grew up with his brothers Abraham J., Simon J., James J., and Ruliff on his father's farm on what is now Waughaw Road, in Towaco, a section of Montville. In his boyhood, he received a rudimentary education in one of the local schools. His practical education came from assisting his father on the farm and tanning hides, making shoes, and providing other services under the direction of his father at the tanyard.

When James felt that his sons were ready to assume full responsibility for the property, which they would ultimately inherit, they were required to pay the taxes. In 1787, Martin J. was twenty-four years old when he paid taxes on fifty-five acres of *un*improved land. By the following year, he had made improvements to the land, when the Martin J. Van Duyne house was built. Records show that the taxes increased. Then in 1811, James Van Duyne bequeathed to his five sons the farms on which they lived, subject to each paying $125 towards a legacy to their four sisters.

In 1789, Martin J. Van Duyne built his house perpendicular to the dirt road that existed in the 1700s and later would become the busy U.S. Route 202 that now extends the full length of the East Coast. As was customary during that era, the front of the house was built facing south to absorb the sun's rays for passive heating. The west portion, featuring a small kitchen, once had a Dutch oven. Connected to the kitchen were the stables for horses and cows, which later became the basement. The kitchen-stable-basement area was built into a slope with the kitchen door facing the road at road level. The living room, built over the kitchen-stable area, had its entrance at the top of the slight slope. The attic, not full height, contained the bedrooms.

In 1790, when Martin J. was twenty-seven years old, he married Sarah Van Wagenne, and within ten years they had three sons, Cornelius M., James M., and John M., and two daughters, Catherine and Hetty.

In the 1800s the Van Duynes house doubled its size as the family grew and became more prosperous. They added another large room to the first floor and more bedrooms in the attic. There was a very small dirt floor storage room at the end of the house with a narrow staircase leading to two small rooms. A dirt floor basement extended the full length of the house. Access to the basement was from either the kitchen in the original building or the stairs on the outside of the house. A slanted wood door covered the outside stairwell.

In 1818, Catherine Van Duyne died less than two months after her son Hiram's birth on July 15. She was one month shy of her twenty-first birthday. Apparently his grandparents, Martin J. and Sarah Van Duyne, and his aunt Hetty cared for the infant. Hiram lived in the old homestead the rest of his life.

In his will Martin left his homestead farm of 82.61 acres to his two unmarried children, James M. and Hetty, with the condition that the house eventually would go to Hiram. Hiram was married three times. His third wife, Ellen Black, gave him three children, James M., Hetty, and Sarah Virginia (Jennie).

On July 5, 1861, after his sister Hetty died, James M. Van Duyne, son of Martin J., conveyed to Hiram—his nephew, son of his sister Catherine—all rights to the house and land. In his will, Hiram left the property equally to his son James M. and Sarah Virginia (Jennie), his unmarried daughter. The property remained in joint possession for twenty-five years. James M. lived in one of the New Jersey suburbs, while Jennie lived in the original 1789 portion of the house. When James M. died on April 3, 1917, his wife Flora and their six children conveyed all their rights, title, and interest in the property to Jennie Van Duyne, who became the sole and last owner of the house.

Jennie Van Duyne continued living in the old house, occupying three rooms and the basement in the westerly portion of the house, and renting out the remainder from time to time to various tenants. To ensure the privacy of the two living areas, the door between the two large rooms was locked on Jennie's side. In the basement a wood wall separated the two sides. The entrance to Jennie Van Duyne's half of the house was over an open porch with white bench seats built into the railing. A second entrance, at the eastern side was through a less-stylish, horizontally split door called a Dutch door.

The house remained in the Van Duyne family for one hundred sixty-five years.

*   *   *   *

Once we settled into the house, Dad set about constructing a series of buildings in the back. First, he built his work shed, followed by the garage for his truck (he had already sold our Chevrolet sedan) and a separate building for the chickens and goats that my parents planned to buy and raise. My dad constructed the chicken coop to separate the chicks from the adult chickens. The goats had one large shed that contained the stable, a milking stand, and a long feeding bin. In front of the shed was a fenced corral. Still further back on the property, Dad dug into the Morris Canal towpath embankment to make a root cellar to store potatoes, onions, turnips, carrots, and apples so we would have fresh food through the winter.

Our new neighbors, also living on small farms, helped my parents survive in their new situation. They taught my parents how to buy, raise, and slaughter the animals. They also taught them how to can food on a large scale. By watching the interaction between our neighbors and my parents, I learned that farmers, as a class, work together. In that respect, I became aware of how small a community we lived in, even though in some cases the farms were quite a distance apart.

The owners of the Vreeland Farms had a peach orchard on the other side of the Morris Canal bed. Dad asked for permission to enter their peach orchard and collect the drops. This was perfect because the fruit was free, ripe, and ready for eating or canning.

Across U.S. Route 202 was an old black walnut tree. The walnut meat was encased in two, very thick, hard coverings. The outside layer had a green skin and, if broken, the liquid inside would severely stain the hands. My parents wore gloves when picking up the nuts from the ground. Then they would cast the nuts on our driveway and drive the truck over them to break off the outer skin. Breaking through the next layer—the hard thick hulls—took effort and required hammers and a large iron block Dad gave us. Mother and I would sit on the concrete steps Dad built between the kitchen and the living room and hammer the hulls to extract the meat. The yield per nut was small, but the meat was delicious eaten alone, with raisins, or in the fruitcakes Mother baked. I looked forward to the time Mother and I spent cracking those black walnuts.

There was ample land for Dad and Mother to farm. In addition to raising chickens and goats, they grew a variety of vegetables that we ate immediately, canned and stored in the basement of the house, or put in the root cellar. The acre of land on the other side of the driveway and the row of trees was our garden. Dad plowed it and both parents_prepared to plant potatoes, onions, turnips, carrots, tomatoes, green peppers, green beans, corn, and white and red radishes for us, as well as big cow beets for the goats. One of my delights was breaking off a rhubarb stalk, from the plants behind the house, peeling it, and eating the tart fruit.

On one of our neighbors' farms there was a slow-moving stream in which watercress grew in abundance. The plants would thrive in inlets where the water was always fresh but had little movement. With the permission of the farmer, Mother and I would go with two galvanized buckets and two pair of scissors to harvest the watercress. We cut the stems at water level, leaving the roots to grow a new crop. Once home, we would wash the leaves to remove any sand. All three of us would eat thick watercress sandwiches with gusto.

Mother sold chickens, eggs, and goat's milk most of the year. There were some mothers who would buy the goat's milk regularly because their children could not digest cow's milk. We also had a buck that would mate with the does a certain number of weeks before Easter, giving the kids ample time to grow fat so they could be sold in the spring to Italian families for their Easter celebrations.

After moving to the farm, I made it known that I was not going to drink goat's milk. I was having lunch at a neighbor's farm when I announced that I only wanted to drink their cow's milk since I knew they raised both animals. The wife pacified me, but after I finished my second glass, I was informed of the trick: I was enjoying goat's milk. I still do.

My parents bought a machine that separated the curd—the fat in the goat's milk—from the whey—the thin watery part of the milk. The machine had its own table, standing three to four feet high. There was a series of small cylinders inside through which the milk passed. Once the curd and whey were divided, Mother would let them stand in the icebox until the whey curdled to make pot cheese. Mother also used this process to make butter. She would mix yellow food color into the fat—the taste would not change, but yellow butter looked more appealing than white butter. We would either eat the pot cheese as one would eat cottage cheese, or she would make her famous cheesecake. When my cousins visited they raved about it, which made her proud. Their accolades made me proud of her, too.

Mother also ground flour out of wheat kernels that came in large sacks. Nothing went to waste in our house, so the emptied white or flowered sacks made of soft cotton became our pillowcases. But before she began grinding, she washed the kernels several times. In the first wash, some wheat hulls would surface. She skimmed them off. When she was satisfied with the cleanliness of the kernels and that all the hulls were removed, she would put a thin layer of kernels on a cookie sheet and toast them in the coal stove. The next step was the grinding.

Mother would then fasten a large cast-iron grinder to the side of the kitchen table. It had a very large handle, which gave the grinder better leverage to mash the kernels. The dies used ranged in size. The small size was used to create fine flour for pancakes, bread, and cakes, and one of the larger dies ground the wheat for cereal. To make the process easier, she always used the larger die first and then put the flour back through using the smaller die. I would sit at the table and watch the white powder come out of the opening at the side of the grinder. I begged her to let me turn the crank; and when she finally gave me the opportunity I could not move the handle. We both laughed. When I was older, I had the strength to help her, and, in some cases, I would prepare the flour myself.

The syrup that we used on our pancakes came from the berry bushes in the woods behind the house or from the peaches collected from the Vreeland Farms, all of which Mother canned. She even wore boy's high-top boots to protect her ankles from scratches when she gathered the wild berries.

Working the farm was hard on Mother. Dad worked along with her when he came home at night and on weekends, but the care of the animals fell mostly on her. Because her hands were exposed while feeding and milking the goats, her cuticles would crack and bleed in the wintertime. She would apply camphor-ice to them and wear white gloves to bed.

As hard as Mother worked to sell the produce from the farm, her family was the main consumer of the results of her toil. The goats provided meat and milk, and, from the milk, she made butter and pot cheese. The chickens provided meat and eggs. Then there was the very large vegetable garden that she and Dad planted, cared for, and harvested. It was not uncommon to have meals that came entirely from their labors on our land.

I loved living on our farm. I collected eggs from under the hens. I played with the goats and helped Mother feed them. I even learned how to milk the does. Later, when the does freshened (gave birth) I would play with the new kids. Once, when I was about ten and my parents were not home I assisted a doe in the birth of her kid. I removed the film from the face of the kid, cleaned it up, and moved it to the warm kitchen where I bottle-fed it the heavy, brownish milk from the doe. I scooped up and discarded the doe's afterbirth, fed her fresh alfalfa, gave her water, and milked her. Since my parents' intent was to fatten the kids to sell them for meat and to continue getting milk from the doe, we immediately separated the babies from the mothers and bottle-fed the kids until they could drink from a pail.

I have no idea what I might have missed by having not grown up in the suburbs, but I do know that on the farm I had more freedom for unsupervised adventures, and, in the case of helping the doe in giving birth, I had an opportunity to fill in for my parents.

*   *   *   *

After we had settled into our new home I started visiting Jennie. In our house we called her Jennie, but I always addressed her directly as "Miss Van Duyne." Although she was pleasant to me, I felt she never wanted me to stay long. Jennie was a spinster and probably did not know how to relate to a small child. She was sixty-nine years old when we moved into her house. I didn't know anyone so old, so frail, and so wrinkled. She showed me some of her possessions and always had cookies for me.

As our landlady, Jennie never gave my parents any difficulty. Mother would give her fresh vegetables and fruit and, to my delight, I had the task of delivering them. It was another excuse to enter her quarters, which held a never-ending fascination for me because of the old things she had lying about.

*   *   *   *

During the Great Depression, many men left their homes and families to travel from town to town looking for work. They were honorable men caught up in circumstances beyond their control. Some were blue-collar workers; others might have been professionals. They would stop at "hobo communities" along the way, where they could sleep and feel a degree of protection. These traveling men would "mark" houses along their route to indicate either a helpful or hostile homeowner. One mark was a sleeping cat. We never saw a mark on a tree or telephone pole, but men stopped at the house in the morning asking to do some work in return for breakfast. Mother did not put them to work but always gave them food. They would sit on the glider swing in the backyard to enjoy their pancakes, three eggs sunny-side-up, homemade goat sausage, fried potatoes, and bread, as well as several cups of coffee. Seconds were available if they wanted them. I had the pleasure of serving the men. Mother's action taught me a valuable lesson. She modeled how to be kind to a stranger in need.

By contrast, there was one man who came to the door and asked, "How's about something to eat?" This did not sit well with Mother, and she refused him. When jobs were available during World War II, and the traveling men disappeared from the roads, we saw this same man on the streets of Boonton and figured he was a "professional traveling man." From then on, every time we saw him we called him "How's About."

*   *   *   *

Mother's focus was not only on providing the food to sustain her family but also on my education. In January 1935, a month after my fifth birthday, she enrolled me in Linwood School, which was built in 1907 and located a short distance east of our house. Even though Mother was told the year started in September, the principal allowed me to stay. The school had two large rooms with multiple grades in each room. In each room, there was a large coal-wood stove for heat during the winter months. The toilets were outside, causing some degree of hardship in cold weather. The students at Linwood were the children who lived too far from the Montville Public School, located at the corner of Main Street (U.S. Route 202) and Taylortown Road. We walked to Linwood School with the protection of an older student who wore a colored vest indicating he was a school walking guard.

That summer Linwood School closed, and we all transferred to the Montville Public School, about two miles from my house. (As of this writing the Linwood School building is being used by local seniors for their activities.) I went into the second grade having spent only a half a year in first grade. This school building had a science laboratory, a cafeteria, an auditorium, a nurse's office, inside restrooms, and a principal's office. It also had a classroom with its own cloakroom for each of the eight grades. I rode a school bus since it was too far to walk.

I loved school. I cried when it ended for the summer, and I looked forward to September when school started again. I am sure part of this was because school gave me the opportunity to play with more children than lived near my house. My excitement at finding new playmates was part of the reason I talked during class. My punishment was to stand in the first-grade cloakroom. It seemed this was the standard disciplinary action. This was the first and only time I was so disciplined. Mother told me of a boy who rebelled against this treatment. In acting out his rebellious side, he used his penknife to cut the buttons off all the garments that were hanging on pegs in the room. Unfortunately for his mother, who had the task of sewing them back on, the boy cut some of the cloth as well.

As much as I missed school during the summer, outdoor activities helped to fill the summer months. The Van Duyne house was a distance from where my classmates lived, so, as an only child, I had to find creative ways to amuse myself when I was young. I did this with imaginary friends, my dogs and cats, or just myself. When I was a little older, Mother would let me walk to my friends' homes with instructions to never accept rides from strangers.

From an early age I loved being in water. To satisfy my desire, Dad dammed up the brook that ran behind the house so I had my own private swimming hole, however shallow, any time I wanted to cool off.

For real swimming, however, I would spend either a day or a week at Aunt Lotty and Uncle Henry Buesing's cabin on Lake Hopatcong, an hour's drive northwest of our house. Mother had two other brothers, Willy and Justus, who lived in Secaucus. They also had summer cottages at the lake. Their wives and younger children stayed at the lake during the summer months while my uncles and their older children returned to their jobs in the city during the week. We loved swimming, but another pleasure we had at the lake was taking out the row-boat and, while still in the boat, collecting blueberries from the bushes hanging over the water. Aunt Lotty would use them to make blueberry pies.

Another of our summer activities took place at the R. H. Doremus House. Its magnificent barn was diagonally across U.S. Route 202 from our house. In the 1930s Richy Wood's parents owned the property, and the barn became the center of many long hours of enjoyment. I played there with Joey Carnogursky, Bobby Conway, Herby Fox, Marilyn Hamming, Romona Morrow, Wilma Murdock, and Richy Wood. Since this was a farm community, each lived a good distance from me and, in this case, the barn. They either rode their bicycles or walked. I just walked across the road.

The barn was in good condition and was safe for our play. The hayloft on the second floor was the main attraction. We entered through the double doors, walked up a flight of stairs, and then climbed a ladder attached to the platform built over the stairwell. Someone would grab the heavy-duty rope that had a large knot tied at the bottom and would swing it to a willing receiver standing on the stairwell platform. One of us would jump, straddle the knot, and swing over the hay. The next person in line might give the first person one or two swings before jumping on by straddling the legs of the first person. The two would swing until the weight of the second person would force the first one, or more likely both, to fall into the hay. We did this for hours.

When I arrived home, Mother made me undress by the kitchen door so I would not track hay into the house. I had hay in my ears, nose, and hair and all through my clothes. But what fun! She always would ask me the same foolish question, "Why do you play so hard?" I never answered her because she just would not understand. Since Mother's childhood did not allow for quality playtime, she did not understand how serious play could be or how one could become totally committed to it.

*   *   *   *

My cousin Dick Zapf lived in Lincoln Park with his parents, Herman and Jose, and his younger brother, David. They owned one of the houses that Dad had built on Longview Ave. before he went bankrupt. Dick and I were very close. When my parents and I visited their home, I would pass the time in the basement, playing with Dick's elaborate model trains and the miniature towns they traveled through.

Dick taught me how to ride my first two-wheel bike. It was a boy's bike because a girl's bike was too expensive. In one day I learned to maintain my balance, but finally the rutted drive way became my demise. Some of the stones jammed the front wheel and I fell causing a cut in my eyebrow which generated a great deal of blood. When I put my hand up to the cut and saw all the blood, I screamed. I thought I had lost my eye. Both Dick and Mother reassured me this was not the case. Mother put me to bed, and Dick stayed there until I woke up. At the age of eight, thanks to Dick, I could now ride my bike on U.S. Route 202 and expand my social world. I had that bike for several years and took it apart at least twice to paint it. I was always concerned that I had not assembled the bike properly and would not have parts left over.

Part of my social expansion included becoming a Camp Fire Girl under the tutelage of Madeline Mason. She was also my Sunday school teacher at the Montville Dutch Reformed Church. Madeline lived in Lake Valhalla, which meant a two-and-a-half mile ride that included pedaling up a mile-long hill. Madeline lived there with her two daughters, Madeline and Joan, who were also Camp Fire Girls, and her husband, William, who was the superintendent of the Montville school system. William Mason Elementary School on Taylortown Road was later named after him. Madeline taught us to respect nature and enjoy the beauty in our environment. We never camped overnight but would leave our home early in the morning to spend the full day in an area called The Glen around Botts Pond, a short distance from Lake Valhalla. Once we built a fire pit, covered a potato with mud, and put it in the fire to bake. That was a disaster, because the potato did not cook all the way through, but the exercise was fun nonetheless. We collected small plants and arranged them in a covered, empty fish tank. The moisture the plants generated helped keep them alive. This was my first creative gardening experience. We also made Indian beaded jewelry, which we sometimes sold to our neighbors. We also sold flower and vegetable seeds. One neighbor told Mother that she really didn't use the seeds but couldn't resist the sales approach of this cute, energetic girl.

During the winter, the portion of the old Morris Canal bed behind the house became the center of our social life. The yellow school bus dropped off my friends—generally the same ones who played in the barn—at the different bus stops along U.S. Route 202. They would change clothes, pick up their skates, and walk to my house. I was the last one to be dropped off on the route, but by the time they reached me, I was ready. My house was not one of the official bus stops, but since I was always late, the bus driver felt it prudent to pick me up at the house instead of waiting for me farther down the road.

It was still light in the sky when they all walked down my driveway, and we climbed the embankment forming the old towpath that bordered the Morris Canal bed. If it snowed the night before we might have a snowball fight on our way to the canal. When we arrived, however, the snow had to be cleared away before we could skate. Generally, the older boys did this in no time, skating behind wide-scoop snow shovels. If we had to perform the task it might take up most of the daylight, but it would be ready to skate on the following day assuming it did not snow again.

The canal basin that was now our skating rink was about a hundred feet wide to enable the canal boats to turn around or pass one another. On either side of this basin the canal narrowed to about a forty foot width with a towpath on the embankment from which mules once pulled the canal boats. The older boys would use the wider center portion for their ice hockey games, forcing the younger skaters to use the narrow parts of the canal on either side.

I felt the narrow sections were more fun to skate anyway. We would organize races to see who could skate the fastest. Trees lined the canal bed, and their branches formed a canopy. In some cases, the branches touched the ice, which created natural obstacles but also made the area more mystical. After an ice storm the ice-covered twigs and branches transformed the canal into a winter wonderland. The ice was often scattered with twigs, and many skaters fell because of them, myself included. Being a tomboy, I also sprained my ankles jumping out of trees.

We skated until it was dark and very cold and our extremities were nearly frozen. When I walked into the house, Mother would put my feet and hands in lukewarm water to thaw them. She kept asking me the same silly question, "Why do you play so hard?"

*   *   *   *

I felt fortunate to find a copy of The Morris Canal, A Photographic History by James Lee[3], which helped me research the history of the canal. It had ceased to operate in 1924. (I will describe more of the history of the canal in Part Two.) I quickly paged through the book but was unsuccessful in finding something that looked familiar to me. Then I realized the pictures had been taken more than fifty years before I lived in the Martin J. Van Duyne house. Nonetheless, the book was enlightening. *A Hundred Years, A Hundred Miles* by the late Barbara N. Kalata[4] is a scholarly text on the history of the Morris Canal. Mrs. Kalata, a former resident of Lincoln Park, was instrumental in placing the canal on the state and federal registers of historic places.

I did not live in Montville during the time the Morris Canal was in operation. Nonetheless, it was special to me for other reasons. I would lie on my back on the mule towpath for hours dreaming as I looked at the images in the clouds. Lee, on the other hand, extolled his love of the canal through the photographs he collected in his book:

> I think, however, that the Morris Canal was a beauty mark, where men could work and boys and girls could play; a place where a Sunday walk on the towpath was sheer contentment; a place where there were more fish than fishermen; and an engineering wonder that brought visitors from all over the world who stood, marveled at it, and admired it.
>
> The Morris Canal is gone forever. Never again will the sound of the boatman's conch shell horn echo and re-echo in the valleys and throughout the mountains of New Jersey.
>
> The faithful mules and horses that toiled so long and hard pulling the heavy boats also have gone.

On the other side of the canal was a large wooded area that provided ample space for all sorts of adventures. I would start out on my travels with my dog, Scotty, who was a brown and white mutt, and my cat, Midnight, who was solid black with four white paws and followed me everywhere. I would stroll along the brook, cross one of the bridges over the canal, and walk up to the railroad tracks of the DL&W Railroad, which many years later would take me to New York City to work.

Behind our house the Morris Canal and the DL&W ran parallel to one another. As the canal provided the backdrop for my dreams and fantasies as a young child, the railroad became the avenue to start my grown-up dreams of trips I would take when I was older. One of my distinct memories is of evenings listening to the difficulty the freight trains had in climbing the slight grade on ice-coated tracks. The sound of the slipping wheels and the train whistle announcing its approach at the car crossing was truly sorrowful. This sound would wake me up, and I would put a pillow over my head so I would not hear what, to me, was a mournful cry for help.

*   *   *   *

From the time I was six and as long as we lived in the stone house, Mother took me to New York City for my birthday in December. We took the DL&W to Hoboken, New Jersey. From there we transferred to the Hudson Tubes and exited in New York City at 34th Street and Broadway across the street from the R. H. Macy department store. We walked up 6th Avenue to Radio City Music Hall to see the Christmas show and movie for that year, including the performance of the famous Rockettes. We always had lunch at the Horn and Hardarts Automat, which was a pure delight. I put nickels in the slot, the carousel turned around, a door opened, and I extracted the food I had chosen. In the afternoon, we visited one or two of the many museums and historic sites. My four favorite attractions were the Hayden Planetarium, the American Museum of Natural History, the Empire State Building, and the Statue of Liberty.

Visiting the Hayden Planetarium was a predictable excursion. Mother had a fascination with the stars and planets. During the summer or on a winter night, she took me outside to point out the constellations. The planetarium enchanted me not only because Mother was interested in the stars but also because looking up at them was similar to lying on my back along the abandoned Morris Canal bed and seeing shapes in the clouds. She taught me how to find the Big and Little Dippers, Orion's Belt, and the Seven Sisters. During the summer, we marveled at the Milky Way. The stars and planets I saw in the planetarium sky seemed closer than those I saw in the sky from my bedroom window.

We spent hours at the American Museum of Natural History. Each year, we focused on a different section. Mother knew in advance where she was going to take me. She seemed to know her way around, and I stayed close to her fearing that if we ever got separated I would be lost forever. Of all the sections of the museum, I most enjoyed the displays about how the American Indians lived. I was amazed by how they could live in those tents in the winter when I was often cold living in a house.

When I was seven, we first took the elevator up the Empire State Building. The speed took my breath away. When we reached the observation deck and looked down on the other buildings and streets below I felt I had lost my stomach. Mother's hand gave me a sense of security, but that did not transfer to my bodily sensation. No matter how many times I went up the elevator, I loved the speed required to take us to the eighty-sixth floor in less than a minute.

To reach the Statue of Liberty, we had to take an excursion boat from Battery Park across the Upper New York Bay. It was exciting to have the wind sweep past my head as I looked back on the city skyline. To reach the crown (the arm and torch were closed to visitors), we had to climb inside the statue on narrow metal stairs. The sound of all the pounding shoes echoed inside the statue. Even though it was thrilling to be up that high and look out the small windows in the crown I could not wait to get out. I made that climb only once.

Winter brought not only my birthday but Christmas as well. My parents did not have enough money to buy the number of presents many of my school friends received, but my dolls always had new outfits. I do not remember feeling deprived. My aunts bought me sufficient toys and clothes. Our Christmas trees were selected from the many cedar trees in the back of the house. Cedars were denser than the typical trees bought on a lot, so the lights, ornaments, and strips of thin tin foil, which we called rain, were put at the end of the naturally cone-shaped tree. Mother placed a cedar branch on top of the iron stove in the living room, creating an intoxicating aroma throughout the house.

Other smells I associated with Christmas were sawdust, cigar smoke, and oranges—an odd combination of smells. I would spend a few days during the holidays with my godparents who lived above their butcher store in Secaucus. Uncle Fred and Aunt Hanna Buesing worked in the store, which had sawdust on the floor, and the room always smelled of Uncle Fred's cigar smoke. One of my treats was receiving an orange. All three fragrances blended into one beautiful memory.

Part of the enjoyment of my visit to my godparents was when my cousin, Wilma, would take me into New York City to sightsee. I always looked up to Wilma. She was special not only because she was an executive secretary to a president of a major corporation in New York City but also because when we were together she always had time for my questions and was never impatient with me. I remember riding the Hudson Tubes under the Hudson River and suddenly realizing that we were indeed underwater. I asked Wilma what had happened to the fish. She laughed but then explained how the tunnel was built and how safe the construction was. Wilma was ten years older than me. She was old enough for me to want to emulate her but not old enough to be a parent-like figure. For example, I did not like spinach until I found out that she did. From then on, I ate all my spinach. Mother chose Wilma as my middle name, which also added to the closeness I felt for her.

＊   ＊   ＊   ＊

Mother guided my religious training with the same dedication she spent on my historical and environmental education. I was baptized a Lutheran but since there was no church of that denomination in our town at the time, I attended the Montville Dutch Reformed Church on Church Lane.

I enjoyed the Bible stories and became an active participant in Sunday school. I particularly looked forward to Christmas Eve services because we entered the church holding our lit candles. The pastor was the Reverend Donald Wade, and since he did not have children I think he made all of us his children—at least I felt that he thought I was special.

Preparing for church and Sunday school was an important activity in our house. On Saturday night, I had the traditional bath that everyone laughs about, although I had more than one bath a week. My blonde hair was washed and put in rag curlers. In the morning Mother combed my hair into pipe-curls like Shirley Temple wore. Otherwise my hair was always in braids circling my head.

The Montville Dutch Reformed Church was founded in 1756 in Old Boonton. When that village went into decline in favor of a new town site further upstream along the Rockaway River many of the members moved to Montville. The church elders decided to build their next church closer to the homes of the congregation. So in 1818 the sanctuary was re-built on Church Lane, in Montville, across the street from the present church building. In 1856, another structure was built at a cost of five-thousand dollars. Many of the timbers that had been used in the Old Boonton edifice were used again in the 1856 structure, which served the congregation for eighty-two years.[5] Records show the families of Martin J. Van Duyne of Montville and Johannas Kingsland of Boonton were buried in the old cemetery. My parents are buried in the new cemetery.

In the early morning of June 28, 1938, a fire, in all likelihood started by a vagrant sleeping in the back of the chapel, quickly spread to all parts of the church probably helped by heavy winds. The flames completely destroyed the structure.[6] When Walter Doremus, Jr. was interviewed for this book he said he discovered the fire and is still very emotional about it and has vivid memories of the experience.

Walter was returning from an evening class at Consolidated Edison on 14th Street and the East River in New York City. At midnight, he debarked from the DL&W at the Towaco station and saw a glow in the night sky that had to be a fire. He calculated by the size and location that the Montville Dutch Reformed Church was on fire. With his heart in his throat, tears in his eyes, and his adrenaline pumping full force, Walter drove his 1936 Chevy down U.S. Route 202 to Changebridge Road and then to the corner of Church Lane. When he reached that intersection he said he "laid on the car horn." On the left side of the Church Lane was Reverend Donald Wade's house. On the other side lived the Ernest Van Duyne family, who owned the Van Duyne Dairy. Both men opened their windows at the same time and Walter told them of the fire. They called the fire department.

When Walter reached the church the doors were open. He tried to save the old Bible, but the flames were too intense. Neighbors and the volunteer firemen responding to the alarm tried to save articles from the building, including the new pipe organ, but with no more success than Walter experienced. The heat cracked the church bell.

Volunteer firemen staffed firehouses in those days. When a call came to the station, first a siren would be sounded to alert the firemen. This was followed by a set of whistles that signaled the firemen, and everyone else, where to go. Mother had posted a list on the wall showing locations next to the number of whistles. Those sounds were always frightening and sorrowful, but they were downright terrifying at night. All three of us ran outside and looked over the tree line in the direction of the flames dancing in the night sky. Just as Walter knew, we realized our church was burning.

After the debris from the destroyed church was cleared away, members of the Montville Dutch Reformed Church united to quickly build a new structure on the same site. Seed money of $27,500 came from the insurance policy. Another $12,500 was needed to replace the furnishings, organ, church bell, and other equipment. The $12,500 was raised through large and small donations.[7]

The old bell was melted down into smaller bells and sold for ten dollars each to contribute to refurbishing the church. I gave the bell my parents bought to the Montville Township Historical Society.

I have a special memory associated with the bell my parents bought. For years, each Christmas morning, Dad would ring the bell, and when I ran down the stairs, he would say, "You just missed him." He meant Santa Claus, of course. It hadn't occurred to me that Santa was not able to come down our chimney ever since Dad had sealed it off.

*   *   *   *

Although our Christmas celebrations and my trips to New York City with Mother continued, my ideal pastoral life changed. It ended when I heard the Japanese had bombed Pearl Harbor. My cousins Jack and Bob and their parents, Aunt Will and Uncle Jack Wilhelms, were preparing to leave our house to return to their home in Secaucus when I rushed outside to tell everyone what I had just heard on the radio. I did not understand how this would affect my life, but Dad did. He had been in the Navy during World War I.

Each night the three of us listened to the news and tracked the wins and losses of our armed forces as they fought on two fronts to protect our country and the world from fascism. President Franklin Roosevelt asked all of us, regardless of age, to sacrifice and support the war effort, which we did gladly. Everyone hung black shades on their windows and pulled them down at night and painted black paint over half of their automobile's headlights. Both of these precautions were to prevent excessive illumination that could attract enemy planes at night. We bought Victory Bonds. Dad went to work on the graveyard shift building ships at Kearny Shipyards along the Hackensack River. Mother joined a first-aid volunteer group to learn how to treat injured persons if the enemy ever invaded us. Often Mother recruited me as one of the pretend casualties. Men and women were alert all night watching for enemy aircraft, and, of course, women entered the factories to build war equipment while men fought overseas.

Gasoline was rationed, although the primary need for conservation was not gasoline but rubber tires since the Japanese had seized plantations in the Dutch East Indies that produced ninety percent of America's raw rubber. The national maximum "victory speed" of thirty-five miles per hour was enforced to conserve both rubber and gasoline. Various stickers were affixed to windshields, depending on the official needs of the driver. An A sticker was issued to owners whose use of their cars was nonessential. This category would qualify drivers for three to four gallons a week. Those driving with B stickers, eligible for eight gallons a week, were classified as essential to the war effort. In addition, there were three special classes of drivers. The C stickers indicated physicians, ministers, mail carriers, and railroad workers, while T was for truckers and X for members of Congress and other VIPs. We had both A and B stickers.

Food and other items were not exempt from rationing. Every family was issued a War Ration Book dictating how much food any one person could buy as well as how many items were considered essential for the war effort. Neighbors planted "victory gardens" to grow their own food; we were already doing that. Standing in line to buy items that were rationed was a normal occurrence. I stood in line to buy my father's Phillies cigars, which cost five cents each; he would smoke one every morning on his way home from work just to keep himself awake. Children saved tinfoil and tin cans that were flattened once the ends were removed.

Mother was especially concerned about whether or not she would be allowed to buy enough sugar for her canning, since it was a critical ingredient. Somehow this always worked out for her. She was also interested in buying a good pork roast—a meat we did not raise. She accomplished this by having me request the meat. She was convinced I could get a better cut of meat from the butcher than she could. Whether or not it was true, that was my assignment, and I liked it.

Each year, the draft age increased and finally reached the point at which we were afraid that Dad could be drafted at age forty-four even though he was a veteran of World War I. We prayed that the war would end soon or that his working in the shipyard would qualify him for a deferment. The war was all consuming. Mostly, people were patriotic and supported President Franklin Roosevelt. The attack on Pearl Harbor unified America in a war effort of a magnitude not seen since.

During those four years, sixteen of my male cousins went into the service. All returned. One cousin, George Buesing, received two purple hearts in the African campaign, one while serving under General Patton's command and the other under General Clark's command. Another cousin, Henry Buesing, was in a prisoner of war camp for a short time. During those years, the dinner table was a time to discuss the war, American politics, and the safety and location of my cousins. As a young child, I was immersed in the political discourse that had a great influence on me during my adult years.

I lived in the stone house for seven of the twelve years of the Great Depression and one of the four years of World War II—not the best of times for America. During the Depression some men left their families or committed suicide. Dad did not question his role as the provider for his family and worked very hard at menial jobs to support us and pay his debts. It was not until the outbreak of World War II that Dad received a good steady wage by working at the Kearny Shipyards. These hours gave him the time during the day to build a house in Boonton, the last house he would build and the last one we would all live in together.

In the summer of 1944, we moved to Boonton where I entered Boonton High School as a freshman.

Major Changes to
the Martin J. Van Duyne House

Ten years after moving from the old stone house, while I was living in California, major changes were starting to unfold in the life of the Martin J. Van Duyne house. First, after the Van Duyne family had owned the house for 165 years, in 1954, Jennie Van Duyne consented to sell the one-acre lot on which the house stood to Robert and Margaret Benson, but there was one stipulation. The Bensons agreed to Jennie's retaining occupancy of her half of the house during her lifetime. Approximately a year later, on August 28, 1955, Jennie died at age ninety. Entering into this contract demonstrated the Benson's patience and love for both Jennie and the house. They were determined not to allow anyone else to buy it. They knew it had to be theirs.

Once the Bensons took full possession, they began extensive remodeling. They extended the roof of the house in a long sweep creating a porch across the south face of the house.[8] They removed my cherished porch—the open porch that Jennie had used to enter her portion of the house. And they sealed off my beloved well. Finally, they built a two-car garage that they attached to the house with a breezeway.

Certainly these changes enhanced the livability of the house, but they destroyed the authentic design of the structure. When I first saw the results, I wanted to cry. What did they do to the beautiful house of my youth? To preserve the history of this building, I gave many pictures of the house from before the remodeling to the Montville Township Historical Society to display in their museum.

Luckily, the Bensons renovated the interior of the house without altering the colonial design. They replaced the warped flooring with new floors, installed forced air heating, and modernized the kitchen. They built a full bathroom in what was once my bedroom and added indoor stairs to reach the basement.

In 1958, the next milestone took place when the house became the focus of a successful preservation effort, forcing the realignment of Interstate 287 to avoid demolition of the structure. With the support of their neighbors and the influence of then-State Senator Thomas J. Hillery, the Benson Family was successful in having the line of the highway changed.[9] The Bensons saved the house, but the down side was that the embankment of the highway was in their front yard. It was built over what was once our large vegetable garden. (Interstate 287 runs in a crescent from Mahwah, New Jersey, at the New York State border south to Perth Amboy, New Jersey.)

In 1966, Richard and Jean Chipman bought the house from the Bensons and lived there for thirty-seven years. I visited them three times. The first time was with Dad in 1970 and then alone in 1998. Richard died in May 2002, and Jean died in January 2003, three months after my last visit.

In August 2003, Paul Lum purchased the Martin J. Van Duyne House from the Chipman estate.

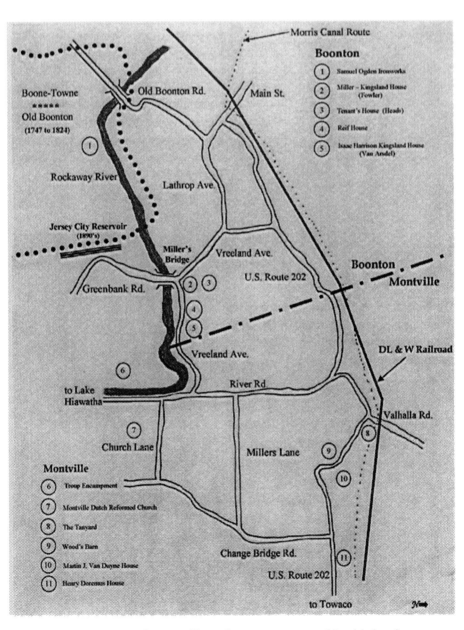

The portion of Montville and Boonton covered in this book.

One of the first things Dad did after we moved into the Martin J. Van Duyne house was to hang a swing from a maple tree on the east side of the house. Looking at the house, the kitchen window is on the bottom, the window directly above that is my parent's bedroom and my bedroom (not shown) would be on the left. (In June 1937, I was 6 1/2 years old.)

In March 1938, Dad and I are feeding three young goats in front of the barn that was destroyed by the September 12, 1939 hurricane.

I am drawing water from the 'old well. (July 1940, I was 9 ½ years old)

The last of the March 1941 blizzard. The maple tree in the foreground fell in a 2001 storm. The tree provided shade for generations of Van Duynes.

In the summer of 1941, I am sitting on the porch to the entrance to Jenny Van Dune's portion of the house. This beautiful porch was removed in the late 1950s when the house was renovated.

Mom took this picture of Dad and me after we raised the flag on Memorial Day 1942. In the background, past the driveway and one of the last trees in a row, is the vegetable garden, not yet planted. Route 202 runs parallel to the telephone poles on the right. In the background, behind the trees, is a road that crossed over the Morris Canal bed to the Vreeland Farm's peach orchard.

Mom and Dad in front of the Dutch door entrance to the Martin J. Van Duyne house, on January 3, 1943. They were on their way to "The Acres", their newly purchased property in Boonton.

The last snow fall, April 1944, with the well sweep in the background.

The barn of R. H. Doremus House as it looked on October 2002. Many a day "the gang" spent in the barn's hayloft.

I am standing in front of the Dutch door leading into our kitchen. I was twelve years old in this picture. (January 3, 1943)

In September 1946, part of "the gang" is sitting on a wall near the Greenback Road Bridge and our swimming hole. From the left to right are Herby Fox, Ruth, Romona Morrow, Wilma Mudrock and Joey Carnogursky.

As an adult my height takes up the whole door. (October 2002)

Robert and Margaret Benson, bought the Martin J. Van Duyne house in 1954 from Jenny Van Duyne after which they made major change to the outside of the house. In 1958 the Bensons petitioned to save the house when it was scheduled to be demolished in order to build Interstate 287. Richard and Jean Chipman owned the house when this picture was taken in 1970. (Taken from the bank of I-287)

Jean and Dick Chipman in from of their home, taken October 1998.

The Bensons raised the roof and extended it over what was to become a porch the full length of the house. The cover to the stairway to the basement remained.

Our Vreeland Avenue, Boonton house is partially hidden by the row of maple and pine trees. The picture was taken close to Vreeland Avenue across the large open field in front of the house.

The back of the Boonton house across the brook and next to the majestic oak tree. The garage was on the right, then the kitchen and master bedroom, followed by the living room with its fireplace. My bedroom was on the left.

This is the way the Boonton house looked in October 1998

In the background is the Isaac Harrison Kingland house once owned by Fredrick and Thelma Van Arsdale. Alexandria Owen, Thelma's grand-daughter and her family live there now. The trees were being cleared away to make room for five new houses. (October 1998)

After the trees had been removed, the beauty of the Isaac Harrison Kingsland house emerged. (October 2002)

The current structure of the Miller-Kingsland House was built in four stages. The first wing, in the foreground, was built in 1740. The gamble roof addition with its small roofed porch was built in 1808. The kitchen wing, not visible in either picture, was added in the late 1920s.

Alex and Mae Ersking Fowler bought the house in 1940. In 1998, the Fowlers added another wing (to the right of this picture) with a bedroom-living room and bathroom to accommodate Alex's physical limitations.

Mae Erskine Fowler, when I visited her in October 2002. Her body was giving out, but her mind was sharp as a tack and there still was much life in her.

At the intersection of Change Bridge Road and Route 202, in Montville this sign marks where the Morris Canal once flowed. Morris County placed signs at every Morris Canal Crossing and feature.

This is one of the many signs placed by the Morris County Heritage Commission along the route of the old Morris Canal.

Part Two

The Miller-Kingsland Tract, Boonton, New Jersey

1944 to 1954

In 1944, my parents built their last home. It was on Vreeland Avenue in Boonton close to the border of Montville. The street was named after one of the early settlers in Boonton, Johannes Vreeland, whose house was halfway up the hill.

Access to our new property was through two stone pillars on the west boundary of the Alex and Mae Erskine Fowler property and down a long dirt driveway lined with fully grown maple trees. At the end of the driveway, midway on the property, was a knoll. This was the spot my parents chose to build our permanent house.

It appeared that another house was to have been built on the knoll. Everything would lead to that assumption, including the two stone pillars marking the entrance and the placement of the trees so large they must have been planted fifty or so years before my parents bought the land. That would have been around the time Anna Heard Kingsland bought the big house from her brother Wilbur. In addition to the maples, and very large pines stood on the front part of the knoll, and oak and maple trees surrounded it. A dirt roadway ran in front of the knoll and over the brook to connect the two old houses, but it was not used when we lived there.

The first half of our new property contained these artfully planted trees with an acre-and-a-half cleared field in front of the knoll adjacent to Vreeland Avenue. The remaining portion had a thick cover of brush, small trees, and brambles that my parents removed. Whatever was cut down was stacked uniformly to be used for the roadbed they were making that would ultimately reach the end of the property, where the temporary house would be. This undertaking required building an earthen bridge using a very large concrete conduit that Dad placed in the brook to both provide a base for the structure and ensure an uninterrupted flow of water. When the foundation was complete Dad had truckloads of coarse gravel unloaded and graded to create the driveway to the temporary house.

Once the brush was completely removed, we discovered the full extent of the brook's meandering. The brook ran on an angle from the upper-left corner of the property, flowed behind our future house, along the Van Arsdel's driveway, serving as a boundary line between both properties, went under Vreeland Avenue, and finally emptied into the Rockaway River. Unlike the unseen stream at the Jennie Van Duyne property, this brook became an integral visual part of the landscape. In the summer, the brook also became an important part of our Irish Terrier Duffy's life. After he chased the birds and in general ran around, he'd lay down in the brook to cool off.

Three lilac bushes grew close to the brook; two were lavender and one was white. Their pungent aroma filled the air, and we looked forward to their blossoming each spring. Next to the lilacs was a majestic oak tree that took command of the property once the brush was removed. It provided shade in summertime, and its leaves displayed a full range of colors during the three seasons. In the winter, ice or snow covered its branches and twigs, adding to its splendor. I loved that tree, though I could not climb it. Dad found a spring close to the foot of the old oak and had a well dug to provide water to the temporary house and later to the house he built on the knoll.

It took both my parents more than a year to clear the land and for Dad to build the temporary house because he was still working the midnight shift at Kearny Shipyards. The permanent house had to wait until after the end of World War II when building supplies became available and he had more money. We moved into our temporary home in the summer of 1944 before I entered Boonton High School. The war in the Pacific and Europe was still raging, Dad was still working at the shipyards, and I was becoming a young lady.

*   *   *   *

In 1707, William Penn made a concentrated effort to increase the number of settlers in Pennsylvania. He traveled to the Lower Palatinates of Germany in the lower Rhine area where he encouraged the inhabitants to migrate to his colony. He told them they could establish homes and farms on fertile land. Thirteen thousand Palatinates gathered to come to the New World. There were so many that they waited for months for passage on a ship and had to endure a shortage of food and lodging in London, England.[1]

One of them was thirty-six-year-old Adam Miller, who arrived in New York with his family on June 10, 1710. The Millers had two girls, ages twelve and six, and one boy, Johannes, age eight. Instead of going to Pennsylvania, however, they first settled in the Ramapo Tract near Saddle River, New Jersey. (Saddle River is near Interstate 287 just south of the New York State line and about twenty miles west of the Hudson River.) In 1720, Johannes married Catrina Straight. Over the next twenty-two years the couple had eleven children. In 1728, Johannes relocated to Morris County. The property he bought would later be in the town of Boonton.

The land that would become Kingsland Farms can be traced back to 1715 as part of a 693-acre tract owned by Richard Bull. According to Alex Fowler's *Splinters from the Past: Discovering History in Old Houses*, "This tract was bound on the south by the Roughaway River (now called Rockaway River) and Church Lane; on the east by the line of Change Bridge road; on the north by the line of U.S. Route 202, where it was intersected by Change Bridge Road, and extended in a straight line to a point a little west of River Road; on the northwest by a straight line to Rockaway River near the present Jersey City Reservoir dam."[2] In 1721, Bull sold the entire tract to John Ready. In 1728, Ready sold 231 acres, or one third of this tract, to Johannes Miller.

In true pioneer fashion, Johannes Miller, his wife, and his first four children carried their worldly possessions in a covered, ox-drawn wagon, most likely following Indian trails until they found the land they wanted to settle. After they located the rightful owner and once the financial and legal arrangements were completed, they built a crude log cabin to satisfy the family's immediate needs. Then all able bodies were used in clearing the land and preparing it to raise crops and farm animals. Later, they built a better house and would even add to that as family requirements increased. This is similar to what my parents faced 216 years later when they cleared and developed five acres of the land once owned by Johannes Miller.

Twelve years later, in 1740, the better house was completed—the first half of what would later become the Miller-Kingsland house. It was comprised of one room on the first floor with a large, cooking fireplace and beehive oven. The small attic had less than ample headroom. In those days it was typical to build a one-and-a-half story house for tax purposes, since the house would be considered to have only one floor. The house also featured a Flemish roof that extended over a porch.

A few miles from the Miller farm on the other side of the Rockaway River was a colonial village called Boone-Towne and later Old Boonton. Built around the Samuel Ogden ironworks, the mill was distinguished for its forges and rolling and slitting mill, which flourished from 1747 to 1824.

Thomas C. Willis, who as a boy and young man lived in Old Boonton, wrote the following in a memorandum in 1859:

> In 1795 there was a rolling mill and a saw mill, standing in the woods on the east bank of the Rockaway River. On the west bank of the river was a large potash factory, a nail cutting mill, a gristmill and a blacksmith shop. A large building, containing eight refining furnaces, stood where the forge now stands. The pig iron, made at the Mt. Hope and Hibernia blast furnaces, was brought here, refined, rolled and slit into nail rods. There were no less than three dams across the river in the neighborhood of Old Boonton at this time.3

During the spring when the rivers swelled with winter snow runoff, water rushed down the Rockaway River and frequently washed out these dams. The owners were constantly rebuilding the dams, hoping the next flood would not destroy them.

Axes, horseshoes, kettles, and iron bars were made at the mill but no ammunition was forged. The iron mill, however, made a significant contribution to the success of the Colonies winning the American Revolutionary War. It is said that the mill's fame came from having forged the links of the iron chain that was stretched across the Hudson River south of West Point to protect the military academy by preventing the British from sailing any farther upstream. Peter C. Wendt, Jr. writes:

> During the Revolutionary War there was considerable military traffic over the more or less parallel roads between Morristown (where General Washington once had his headquarters in the Ford Mansion while his troops were camped in Jockey Hollow) to Pompton Plains on the route to the Ramapos and West Point. One of those roads ran from Morristown, through Morris Plains, and on to Old Boonton, following what is substantially the present U.S. Route 202. Near the village the road descended a fairly steep slope almost to the river, where it then made an abrupt turn to the right, passed through the village and followed the downstream course of the river to Miller's Bridge where Greenbank Road now joins the lower part of Vreeland Avenue. (At this junction the Miller-Kingsland farms were located.) The army followed Vreeland Avenue and River Road, to Montville, where it rejoined U.S. Route 202 and thence to Lincoln Park, and Pompton Plains. It was along that road that Washington routed the artillery and baggage wagons because Miller's Bridge was strong enough to carry the heavy loads.4

As the American Revolutionary War was being fought on Morris County soil it consumed life for the Miller family. In June 1780, the troops of General George Washington encamped across the Rockaway River on what is now the lower part of Knoll Country Club. This tract is where River Road once crossed the Rockaway River leaving Montville and entering Lake Hiawatha.

While the troops were stationed in the area in 1780 General Washington stayed in the Henry Doremus House, a tavern, on what is now U.S. Route 202 as he awaited word about the Battle of Springfield. As of this writing, the Doremus house, built in 1778, has survived intact and unimproved. It has never had electricity, gas, plumbing, or central heating, and no one has lived there for some time. Now owned by Montville Township, the old house is undergoing archeological analysis and restoration.

In 1781, a large portion of General Washington's army and the whole of the elite French corps under Count Rochambeau crossed through the Boonton and Montville area, over Miller's bridge and then in front of the Miller-

Kingsland house, on their way to Yorktown, Virginia. It was reported to have taken three days to complete this passage. I can imagine the excitement of the Miller family, especially the children, as they watched the troops march in front of their house. The adults must have felt a great deal of pride and concern for the safety of the soldiers, and the young boys' minds must have filled with youthful dreams of being in the army and carrying a gun. I can see the women running next to the line of fighting men to give them food and drink and wish them Godspeed. I can only imagine how that march must have changed everyone's lives.

Seventeen years after the American Revolutionary War was won and seventy years after the property was first bought, Johannes Miller's son, Jacob, sold the remaining hundred-acre Miller farm in two parcels. He sold thirty-two acres on the west side of Vreeland Avenue to Edmund Kingsland and sixty-eight acres on the east side to Edmund's son, Isaac Kingsland, who became the fifth owner of the property we are tracking, as well as the first owner of Kingsland Farms. After selling the land, the Millers moved to Ontario County in upper New York State.

In 1798, Isaac Kingsland married Phebe Sutton in New York and moved his new wife into the Jacob Miller house on the property he had just bought. Seven years later in 1805, Phebe died. In 1807, Isaac married his second wife, Nancy Heard, a widow with six children. Together, they had six more. Twin boys Phineas Heard Kingsland and Edmund Wilkinson Kingsland were the first to be born to the couple.

In 1808, Isaac built an addition to the original house. The large block-shaped structure was more spacious and reflected the increased affluence of its new owner. The first floor had two large rooms and a hall with stairs leading to the second floor, which also had a hall, two other large rooms, and one small room. This building had a gambrel roof and three fireplaces in addition to the one in the old building. The simple exterior feathered-clapboard siding was painted white, and there was a small roofed porch in the front. Isaac Kingsland converted the original room, built in 1740, into a kitchen.

According to historian Alex D. Fowler, Isaac Kingsland bought two slaves in 1803. One was a seventeen-year-old boy, and the other was a twenty-two-year-old man. He paid $250 for each, a sizable amount in those days. When Isaac married Nancy Heard her father gave her a slave girl as a wedding present. The North also had slaves, although they were treated more like servants in these

Dutch communities than they were in the South. The Dutch taught their slaves to read and write, and they were allowed to own a gun. All slaves, however, were "freed absolutely" in New Jersey in 1846, the year before Isaac died. This was fourteen years before the Civil War began.

Further research surfaced the name of Dr. John Grimes, who in 1833 established a medical practice in Boonton. According to Peter C. Wendt, Jr., the doctor's recognition came from his involvement with the Anti-Slavery Society in the State of New Jersey for which he was the secretary and whose headquarters for a time were situated in Boonton. Dr. Grimes published and edited Boonton's first newspaper, *The Monthly Advertiser*, in 1843. It lasted but a few editions. He then published the *New Jersey Freeman* from 1844 to 1850. Both publications served as the organ of the Anti-Slavery Society and to propagate the Abolitionist movement.[5]

The success of the Underground Railroad in Boonton was due to the dedication and organizational skills of Dr. Grimes, as well as the involvement of community leaders, such as William C. Lathrop, John Hill, and Philip Wootton.

In 1824, Old Boonton declined for two reasons. First, the old iron mill was no longer profitable. Second, the Morris Canal, still under construction, would bypass the town. But with the coming of a new iron mill—the New Jersey Iron Company—all was not lost. A site two miles north of Old Boonton, where the Rockaway River flowed over a series of cliffs to form the Boonton Falls, was a desirable place for a mill. The power generated from the canal's eighty foot drop at the great incline plane in Boonton was a major factor in choosing the location. So, too, was the abundant waterpower from the Boonton Falls. The canal offered not only cheap transportation of raw materials but also transportation of the finished product to the markets. When I was in high school, each summer brought a series of drownings as young men pitted their skills against the raging waters generated by the falls. The city took action by dynamiting the falls.

The canal was the brainchild of George P. Macculloch, a Morristown businessman whose dream was to build an artificial waterway in New Jersey between the Delaware River at Phillipsburg (started in 1825) and the Passaic River at Newark (started in 1832). It was extended to Jersey City and the Hudson River in 1836. The prospects of a canal traveling through Boonton and other towns along the proposed route was compelling because of the abundant water from the Rockaway, Pompton, and Passaic rivers, each with its own tributaries. For the Boonton area, a canal would provide a way to get new fuel to replace the depleted charcoal supply.

Unlike the state-financed canals in New York and Pennsylvania, private investors built the New Jersey canals. In 1824, the Morris Canal and Banking Company was formed to finance the project. On November 4, 1831, the first complete canal trip started. It took five days to travel ninety miles.

The venture was not as prosperous as the investors had anticipated, but the canal created opportunities in related areas. Real estate values boomed along the route. Manufacturers enjoyed faster turn-around time on both raw materials and their finished products. The DL&W Railroad and other railroads became strong competitors of the canal. It seemed that trains could provide the never ending search for more efficient and faster means of travel. In 1871, Lehigh Valley Railroad leased the Morris Canal properties for ninety-nine years.[6]

In 1829, the New Jersey Iron Company was chartered by the Legislature. The company first acquired water rights and then bought two hundred acres up the hill from the canal, which became the present town of Boonton. This was where the workers lived. A grid system of streets was formed and divided into fifty-by-one hundred house lots that sold for twenty dollars per lot. The only requirement was that the new owners had to build their own house, worth a few hundred dollars, within a year.[7]

As Boonton became established the Kingsland family grew in stature. In 1847, Phineas and Edmund Kingsland were appointed executors of Kingsland Farms when their father, Isaac, died. The twins were partners in a successful law practice in New York City and did not live on the farm; nevertheless, they supervised its operation. Phineas lived in an elegant house on 57 West 37th Street in Manhattan, where a twelve-story commercial building is now located. In the 1880s, he was comptroller of New York City.

During the Civil War, the twins' younger brother, Isaac Harrison, became a member of the executive committee of the Union League in Boonton. The league supported the "Northern Cause."

In 1870, Phineas, Edmund, and Isaac Harrison, who remained on the farm, built the "big house" on that part of the property bordering Montville. Isaac was fifty-six when he became another Kingsland to own the farm. They constructed a Victorian house in the grand manner of those built in the affluent sections of New York City, although this was a farmhouse. The rooms were elegantly designed, with high ceilings, six-foot windows, and the fine trimmings and moldings popular in that era.

Two stone pillars stood at the entrance of a circular gravel driveway lined with trees that made for a serene approach to the farmhouse, which was perched on a rise 100 yards from Vreeland Avenue. The landscaping around the house was simple, with several grand maple trees and many flowering bushes adding to the aura of privacy.

The main part of this three-story house of brick and stone was covered with cement facing painted white. A broad front porch was topped with a flat roof supported by four carved wooden pillars. Gingerbread detailing adorned the porch and roof peaks. The doorway was eight feet high with glass the full length above the six-foot double doors. A bay window was built on either side of the front door. The front of each bay was comprised of three large twelve-light windows. On each side of the bays was a narrow four-above and four-below window. The porch shaded the two bay windows and the rooms behind them from the southerly morning sun. The windows above the first floor were shuttered.

The interior was equally as impressive. A magnificent mahogany-railed spiral staircase dominated the foyer. To the right was a door leading to the formal dining room and to the left another leading to a casual drawing room. Doors from both rooms led to the kitchen, which ran the full width of the house. A straight staircase from the kitchen led upstairs, giving the servants access to the second and third floors.

On the second floor, a gallery circled the spiral stairs. Two doors on the left of the gallery lead to the light-filled master bedroom, which ran the full depth of the house and featured two six-foot windows in each of the three outer walls. On the right side of the gallery in the front of the house, another door led to a smaller bedroom. A large bathroom took up the rear on the second floor.

The gallery extended to a short hallway in the back of the house, where the straight staircase originating from the kitchen led to the third floor. This level held three bedrooms and another bathroom with a large skylight. All the third-floor rooms had deeply sloping ceilings.

In the mid-1800s, Isaac Harrison lost the property through default on the mortgage payments, but Phineas settled the debts and returned the house to the family. At the same time that Isaac experienced a downturn in his financial fortune the town of Boonton faced a recession. In 1876, the ironworks suddenly closed, forcing workers to leave Boonton and seek employment elsewhere. The town survived and recovered with the coming of the DL&W from the west in 1868. The railroad expanded eastward in 1870, developing commuter service and enabling Boonton residents to work in New York City.

In 1889, another Kingsland brother Wilbur Carroll, a bachelor, became the fourth family owner of the farm. He lived in the big house and commuted on the DL&W to New York City where he practiced as a successful lawyer. Wilbur was driven to the station—either the now-demolished Montville station or the Boonton station—every morning by his stableman in a sparkling runabout buggy driven by a pair of well-groomed horses. (Sixty years later I took the DL&W from Boonton to Manhattan, but my transportation was a six-cylinder Plymouth driven by my dad.)

"In the late 1890's the Old Boonton Tract, along with other properties in that vicinity, was acquired by the Jersey City Water Supply Company for purposes of a reservoir......for $85,000," historian Peter C. Wendt Jr. records. "Preparations for the reservoir included the building of a great dam less than a mile downstream from Old Boonton, and the clearing of the reservoir basin of all buildings, structures, roads and trees. Only remnants of foundations and stone boundary walls were left in the basin. A new bridge was built across the inlet to connect an extension of Washington Street in Boonton to the displaced road to Morristown."8

As Boonton changed, the Kingslands added to their big house. In the 1890s, a clapboard siding wing was added to the dining room side, creating a fifteen by thirty foot living room with two bedrooms above it. The addition required dismantling the chimney in the dining room. A fireplace was added in each new room.

It is not clear why Wilbur sold the big house to his sister Anna Heard Kingsland in 1894 for 6,000 dollars. He may have moved to New York City to be closer to his law practice. He retained some financial ties to the Kingsland farms, though. Mabel Kingsland Byrnes Heard, Anna's niece, lived in the big house before she met and married Cedric Head in 1929. Anna gave the old house to Mabel and her new husband as a wedding present, along with one thousand dollars to refurbish it. The old house was in very bad condition and in need of restoration. The new couple added a kitchen wing to the back of the 1808 addition and returned the all-purpose room in the 1740 wing to its original floor plan. The Heads performed with their Kingsland Marionette Shows in the Northeast much of the time, and the restoration took a long time to complete.

During this time, other modifications were made to the 1890s living room wing of the Isaac Harrison Kingsland house. A kitchen, bathroom, and glass-enclosed sun porch were added, effectively creating an apartment with a separate entrance that has been used as such for many years. The size of the big house increased to almost six-thousand square feet of living space.

Wilbur died in 1930, and Anna died in 1933. Mabel (Heard) Head and her husband Cedric inherited the whole property and became the sixth and last of the Kingsland family to own the farm. When the Heads finally finished the restoration of the Miller-Kingsland house, they lived there for only two years before deciding to lease it. They preferred to live in the tenant's building behind the main house and converted the carriage house into a studio where Cedric worked on his creations. The marionettes were large and beautifully dressed and would be hung from poles strung across the studio to keep their wires from tangling. The studio smelled of wood, paint, and glue. I loved it when the couple was home and I could see the marionettes in action. Sometimes they staged a show in their studio, and Cedric would show me how to operate them.

The Heads leased the Miller-Kingsland house to Alex and Mae Erskine Fowler until 1940, after which they sold the house and five acres to them—two-and-a-half acres on either side of Vreeland Avenue. They also sold the Isaac Harrison Kingsland big house and 4.6 acres to Fredrick and Thelma Van Arsdel. In 1943, the Heads sold the five acres between these two houses to Bill and Marie Reif, my parents. The Fowlers had three children—Mae Erskine (Erkie), Susan (Su), and Alexander Jr. (Alex)—who are all still living as of this writing. The Van Arsdels had four children—Lois, Nancy, Elizabeth, and Fredrick. Lois has since died. I am an only child. I played with Erkie, Su and Nancy and was often in their homes.

*   *   *   *

Our temporary house had two floors. The first was split down the middle from end to end with living quarters in the front half and Dad's shop and work storage area in the back half. The living quarters on the first floor included a large kitchen and pantry, a coat closet, and a bathroom. The second floor had two big bedrooms with large closets and an office for Dad. My bedroom faced south toward the front of the property, giving me an unobstructed view of our five acres and the construction of our new home. I still had the same furniture that was in the stone house, plus bookshelves and a larger desk that Dad built for me. A large space in the center of the second floor was used as a combined living-dining room. We ate upstairs only on special occasions or when we had more people than could fit around the kitchen table.

The kitchen was the most used room in the house, and the coal stove was one of the main focal points. Mother prepared delicious, wholesome meals on the stove, which also provided warmth for the room and for Duffy and our various cats that slept behind its frame. Perhaps the most important object in the kitchen was the table, where we ate hearty farm-style meals each day. Mother made sure her family was well fed. I have not been able to find lentil soup, stew with green string beans and lamb (hers was made with goat meat), or cheesecake as good as Mother made. Unfortunately, all her recipes have been lost.

The kitchen table also served as the venue for intense discussions about the political issues of the day, the way the government ran our lives, the day-to-day progress of the war, and the status of my cousins who were in the war. I was always eager to take part in the conversations.

Although the house was our shelter and source of human comforts, it was the outside—the land—that appealed to me most. Looking from the living room windows into the wooded hills behind the house gave me a sense of expansiveness. The land also provided me ample acreage to explore with Duffy. The hillside was covered with pine, maple, oak, and every other variety of tree that grew in Northern New Jersey. In the spring, when the other trees burst forth in green the dogwoods would sprout their blossoms, creating a patchwork of white in the natural tapestry of the landscape. This area also was replete with elderberry bushes from which Mother made syrup for our pancakes.

Our farm life continued. The goats and chickens were brought from the Montville farm and housed in new quarters. In anticipation of the move, my parents had already planted vegetables that were harvested during summer and early fall. The routine of canning continued, but not on the scale that took place at the Martin J. Van Duyne house because now my parents had more discretionary income.

My parents were unaware that they had built their house on a deer path between the hills behind our house and the Rockaway River across Vreeland Avenue. When the deer traveled through the trees, we would see their white hindquarters and the white under their tails. Some mornings we would wake up to find round, dry circles left in our front yard from where they had slept. We think the presence of our goats made them feel safe on our property. Or maybe they were trying to reclaim their territory. Often they would stop to treat themselves to Mother's garden. A contest between human intelligence and the instincts of nature ensued. Even when Dad built a very high wire fence around the vegetable plot, Mother still only barely managed to win the battle.

Bob Wilhelms's mother, Aunt Will, was two years younger than my mother. She and Uncle Jack lived in Secaucus and often came to our farm to get relief from the summer heat. Bob, and sometimes his older brother Jack, would spend a few days with us. Once, when we were living in the temporary house, Bob came to hunt. Dad gave him strict instructions that the deer were off limits, although I cannot believe he would have killed a deer anyway. Bob had to be satisfied with hunting groundhogs, which provided a great service to my parents. I did not have a brother, and Bob did not have a sister, so unofficially we assumed those roles for each other.

*   *   *   *

In 1945, the world welcomed the return to peace. Our military men and women came home. The money spent on the war could be used for peaceful endeavors. Building supplies became more available, Dad reestablished his construction business, and his financial situation became whole again. After more than fifty years, there would finally be a house on the knoll. Dad designed it to complement the placement of the existing pines and the brook that passed behind the knoll. As before, Mother was his helper. She had waited fourteen years for Dad to build her another beautiful house. Through all the adversities, Dad maintained his focus—to provide for his family. Mother had picked a winner.

The completion of the new house also elevated my spirits. I finally was living in a house that I was proud to bring my friends to; a house similar to the ones they lived in. The condition of my previous homes had not seemed to bother my friends, but it had bothered me. Although the Martin J. Van Duyne's house provided a unique experience in my childhood, as a teenager—and later as an adult—I was looking for all the conveniences available in the 1940s and

1950s. Now both Mother and I had a home equivalent to the brick house we had had in Lincoln Park.

The exterior of our new house had wide wood siding painted a light gray with darker gray shingles on the roof. An overhang over a small open porch protected the entrance from the elements. A large combination dining-living room with a stone fireplace welcomed visitors. To the right and down one step was a large bedroom with its own bathroom. This became my bedroom suite with all new furniture. Adjacent to the dining room and in front of my bedroom was a porch that ran the full length of my bedroom. To the left of the front door and in front of the house was an average-sized kitchen with a built-in counter that doubled as a breakfast table. To the right of the kitchen and behind the fireplace was my parent's large bedroom with its own bathroom. Beyond the kitchen were two sets of doors and three leading down to a two-car garage. At the bottom of another flight of stairs was a full basement with a large area under the garage where we stored coal for the furnace. Between the kitchen and the bedroom on the first floor, was a flight of stairs leading to a room that Mother used as a sewing-utility room. This room had the same dimensions as the garage. From there a short flight of stairs provided access to a large attic that could have been converted into a room, but we used the space for storage. The walls were painted, but Dad put beautiful wood paneling in the living-dining room, which complemented the hardwood floors. Mother placed two large Oriental rugs in this room.

*   *   *   *

At the bottom of Vreeland Avenue the road veered to the left at Greenback Road near Miller's Bridge. Vreeland Avenue then continued to pass the homes of my neighbors, the Fowlers, the Heads and the Van Arsdels. If you drove down Vreeland Avenue and turned right onto Greenback Road you would cross the Rockaway River over Miller's Bridge, where General George Washington's army had marched. That spot was our swimming hole. The road then passed Knoll Road and the entrance to the Knoll Country Club. It continued to the bottom of the Jersey City Reservoir dam with its administration and maintenance buildings. The huge dam was very intimidating to a young person, and no one ever mentioned that if it were to crack, those of us who were living directly below it or further along the river would have been washed away.

During the summer, most of my friends from the days when we played in Richy Wood's barn in Montville would come over to swim under Miller's Bridge. After heavy rains or when excess water was released from the reservoir, a great amount of water passed under the bridge, and our swimming became more aggressive. We jumped off the bridge or dove from the bank into the rushing water, letting the currents take us downstream. We stopped our forward motion by catching the trunk of a small tree engulfed in water. Then we walked up the side of the river along other partially submerged small trees to repeat the process. Sometimes even I am amazed by what I did for fun when I was young. I wonder if Mother ever knew.

In high school, I was as aggressive about my schoolwork as I was about my play. Though I was only an average student in grammar school, I fared well in high school. For the first time I was treated as an adult, and I thrived on it. Much to the surprise of Mrs. Decker, principal of the Montville Public School, I made the National Honor Society for Civic Studies. Those dinner discussions over politics and war prepared me for the civics class and the Civic Studies award. During one parent open house, Aunt Jose Zapf, one of my mother's younger sisters, walked into my classroom and observed me as I debated a political position. Later she told my parents, "The fruit doesn't fall far from the tree."

Mother did not want me to smoke cigarettes. "Dare to be different," she said. This mantra worked, but not only when it came to cigarettes. In later years, it became a way of life for me. In remembering her statement, I was giving myself permission not to follow the crowd.

As I matured throughout high school, I was much taller than most of the boys I socialized with, and this became very obvious when it came to dancing. It also seemed as if my height prevented the beat in my head to travel all the way down to my feet. What I needed was a partner who could lead, which was something the boys that age generally did not do well. These shorter boys, with their own inadequacies, had difficulty leading me. To make matters even worse, girls would often dance with other girls since there were never enough boys. In these cases, I generally took the male role which only reinforced my inability to follow gracefully. Learning the jitterbug, however, was the one exception. I was fortunate enough to have had Jimmy Stafford teach me. He was a natural dancer and had rhythm through his whole body. With his hand firmly on my back and a strong grip on my right hand, he threw me into all the moves until he wore me out. It was such fun! The down side of dancing with Jimmy was that he ruined me for jitterbugging with anyone else.

I grew in inches very fast in high school. In fact, I was almost my full height of five feet seven-and-a-half inches by the end of my freshman year. The part of the body that really matters to a girl, however, is the size of her breasts. Sigh! Sigh! I was practically flat-chested. Most of the girls in my situation wore what were called "falsies," foam rubber, breast-shaped extenders that were fastened into a bra. Most times this worked, and my self-esteem was enhanced greatly. On one occasion it was a disaster. Evidently one falsie was not securely fastened to the bra, and during a dance routine I looked down and saw one moving up my chest. I don't know if my partner saw this—how could he not?—but regardless, I was mortified. I ran to the ladies room in tears and tossed both of them in the trash. I wanted to stay there all night.

There was no bus to take me the three miles to Boonton High School (now John Hill Junior High) on Lathrop Avenue so Dad provided transportation when he could during the winter and on rainy days. Otherwise, my transportation was my bike or my legs.

In my senior year, 1947-1948, I wanted to learn how to drive. A friend of mine who had a 1932 Ford agreed to teach me. My father had a 1941 Plymouth. The Ford had a floor gearshift, and the Plymouth had a column gearshift. Since I was not sure which car I would use for my driving test, I learned on both. I just had to visualize the H formation of the gearshifts on the floor of the Ford and then move that up to a vertical position on the right side of the steering post for the column shift. In addition, I had to learn how to synchronize the release of the clutch pedal with the pressure applied to the gas pedal. One evening on our way to a homemade ice cream stand, my friend wanted me to use the long driveway from the temporary house to the street to practice how to manage both pedals. Needless to say, the car jerked forward and then stopped as we made our way down the driveway. My parents watched this movement from the living room window and were sure the Ford was having mechanical problems. Dad put a strong rope in the trunk of the Plymouth, assuming that when they found us they would have to tow the Ford home. When they reached the ice cream stand, my parents learned that their daughter had caused the irregular movements of the car.

One of my first challenges was driving up the very steep and narrow Main Street in Boonton, which followed the Morris Canal's 80-foot drop at the great incline plane, as I described earlier. At the lower end of Main Street was a traffic light on the other side of an even steeper grade—a bridge that spanned the DL&W tracks. If the light turned red when I was on that part of the street I quickly had to move my hands and feet back and forth from the brake, the cutch, the emergency brake and the gearshift to prevent the car from stalling and then to repeat this procedure once the light turns green. It all had to be synchronized so the car would move forward slowly to avoid running into the car in front, and of course you didn't want to roll back into the car behind you. To avoid a collision I had to be sure to have enough space between both my car and the car in front and the one in the rear. This was all done very quickly and soon became second nature. Oh, the joys of driving a stick shift. It's no wonder the automatic shift was invented.

*　　　*　　　*　　　*

From the beginning of high school, I knew I would not go to college but would start working immediately after graduation. Dad was reestablishing his bankrupted business and did not have the money to finance my college education. More importantly, at that time, a college education was not one of my dreams. I wanted to work and earn my own money. Thirty-three years later my objectives changed, and I completed my course work for a master's degree in Organizational Development and Psychology from Antioch University. But in high school, I took business classes and did well in Typing and Bookkeeping, although I barely passed Shorthand. I received good grades, but I worked hard for them, taking many books home and studying long hours at the dining room table. Mother encouraged me in every way she could. She was proud of my accomplishments since she and Dad had not finished grammar school. Instead they had gone to work. I did not have chores during the school year, but, during the summer, I was in charge of the house while Mother spent most of her time outside. She never taught me how to cook. And, oddly enough, my grandmother hadn't taught any of her daughters how to cook, either. When I married, I practiced on my husband.

In my senior year, my classmate Wilma Murdock and I took the DL&W and the Hudson Tubes to Midtown New York to attend Barbizon Modeling School. We both hoped to make modeling a career. It was thrilling for an eighteen-year-old to be part of the mass of commuters all heading to Manhattan to work. Women wore hats and white gloves, and so did I. I felt all grown up.

Upon graduation from high school and modeling school, I tried to obtain a modeling position in the wholesale district but with no luck. The training I had received at Barbizon gave me confidence, though. For the first time in my life, I could walk straight across an unoccupied basketball court instead of walking the circumference. The training also gave me a sense of style and an awareness of my overall appearance. I was a willowy, five-feet-seven-and-a-half-inch young woman breaking out of my environment. I was not ashamed of my background, yet I was yearning for something better—something to which my parents could not expose me.

I had borrowed money from Dad to take the modeling class and wanted to pay him back promptly so that I could be free of debt; therefore, I needed to find employment right away. I found a position as a keypunch operator, the precursor to the computer data entry operator, with Equitable Life Insurance Company on 32nd Street and 7th Avenue. I believe I made fifty-seven dollars a week and worked as much overtime as I could to increase my income. I took the DL&W into Hoboken on the Hudson River, and, from there, I took the Hudson Tubes to 34th Street station. Since my financial situation was very lean, I made all my own work clothes: dresses, blouses, suits, jackets, coats, and hats. I enjoyed designing my own wardrobe and was happy to be able to make my own fashion statement.

Realizing I needed to change companies to receive a wage boost, I found employment with Home Insurance (Fire) Company on Maiden Lane in the financial district in lower Manhattan. Now I crossed the Hudson River by either the Hudson Tubes or the Hudson Ferry. In New York City's early history, before the city had its own fire department, merchants bought insurance from a privately owned fire company. These companies would only put out a fire in a building that displayed their shield.

Working in lower Manhattan was a history lesson in itself. Since I was surrounded by Revolutionary War history where I lived, I had an opportunity to learn even more where I worked—in New York City, where it all started. For current events, dignitaries often came to be honored with a ticker-tape parade riding sorth on lower Broadway from city hall. I was in the crowd, in 1951, cheering General Douglas McArthur after President Harry Truman recalled him from duty during the Korean Conflict. On the day the general addressed Congress and gave his memorable "old soldier's" speech, we heard him through the speaker system at Home Insurance.

Working in Downtown, where the streets are so narrow, provided another unique experience. At 5:00 PM, the offices closed and all employees came down from the skyscrapers and transformed the narrow streets into very wide sidewalks. They walked a short distance, and, like ants, they disappeared into the ground to the various subway stations where trains would take them home.

I loved working in the city, seeing quality theater performances, and shopping in the wide variety of stores. I had the best of both worlds; I worked in a major city with all that it provided yet enjoyed the peacefulness of nature when I returned home. For an independent young woman, this was pure heaven. This must have been the same feeling the Kingsland brothers felt in the late 1800s.

I worked in New York City for five years. It was an exciting time. On the practical side, the money I made gave me a degree of independence, a full hope chest, and ultimately, the finances to buy a Morris Minor—a British, four-cylinder, stick-shift, blue, bug-shaped car. Having my own car gave me the total freedom that only the ownership of an automobile can give.

In 1953, I married, and, the following year, my husband and I moved to Torrance, California, in the South Bay area of Los Angeles. This ended the first chapter in my life and opened up new opportunities in my adopted state.

Recent History of
the Miller-Kingsland Tract

From 1728 to 1944, or for 216 years, two Miller families and six members of the Kingsland dynasty owned the parcel of land chronicled here. Mabel Head, the last member of the dynasty, died in 1950. She was seventy years old. Mae Erskine Fowler died January 29, 2006, at age ninety-nine. She was the last of the three families that bought parcels of land from Mabel.

The exteriors of the three houses have remained much the same, although in 1983 the Fowlers added another wing to the 1808 addition—a bedroom-living room and a bathroom, which my dad built. This was to accommodate Alex Fowler's physical limitations. Mae Erskine also spent her last years in this room.

When I visited Mae in October 2002 she hoped that when the time came someone would buy her beloved house and care for it as she and Alex had. Mae's children are all established in their own states and communities and have expressed no interest in occupying the place.

On July 20, 1991, a fire started in the middle of the night in the Isaac Harrison Kingsland house due to a smoldering ashtray emptied into a wastebasket in what was originally the drawing room. The fire gutted the interior of the main section of the house, including the magnificent mahogany spiral staircase, and the place had to be rebuilt. Only the exterior stone walls prevented the total destruction of the building. Although the interior was completely destroyed, there were neither fatalities nor injuries.

Damage to the main portion was extensive, and the insurance company told Thelma Van Arsdel it would be cheaper to rebuild the interior of the house than raze the exterior walls. Money was limited so she was forced to replace certain architectural details such as wood molding, wooden twelve-light windows, and carved decorative details on the doorways. The third-floor bedrooms were not replaced. The 1890 wing was not seriously damaged in the fire, but was nonetheless extensively renovated using original materials.

Along with new plumbing, heating, and electrical improvements, the living room and apartment wing retained their period authenticity. Sadly, according to Alexandria Owens the current owner, the main portion of the house has a different floor plan than before the blaze. Even the exterior shows some updating; for example, the new building code required a railing on the porch. The third-floor bedrooms were not replaced.

Thelma Van Arsdel died in April 1996, leaving the property to her three surviving children. Everyone wanted to keep the property in the family, but none of the three children or ten grandchildren could afford to purchase the other family members' stakes in the estate. In the end, all the inheritors arranged to sell the dormant front acreage to a developer, allowing a family member to purchase the house on the remaining 1.6 acres. The complicated deal involved the planning boards of Boonton and Montville and finally was settled in September 1998. At that time, Michael and Alexandra Owens (Lois Van Arsdel's daughter) bought the house from the Van Arsdel estate. They have two girls, Gillian Alexandra and Catharine Elizabeth, to continue the Van Arsdel dynasty.

Now the front yard is a short cul-de-sac called Green Briar Court, and there are five additional houses encircling it. "The Van Arsdel home has pride of place at the back, being on a rise and by far the most charming of the homes," Alexandra said. "The community both mourns and celebrates the new construction because a gem formerly hidden by scrub woods is now available for all to see from Vreeland Avenue." One week after the closing of the sale in 1998, Gillian Alexandra Owens was born, making her the fourth generation of Van Arsdels to live in the house on Vreeland Avenue.

When I was in Boonton in October 1998 the large trees and brush in front of the Isaac Harrison Kingsland house were being removed to build the new homes. When I returned four years later, five large residences had been built with the big house directly in the center. Four of them are in Boonton and one in Montville. Although I hated to see the trees removed, selling the land in front of the house secured the future of the Isaac Harrison Kingsland house and kept it in the Van Arsdel family.

I am pleased with how the developer of our property arranged the houses on our five acres after Dad sold it in 1970. The developer built eight other houses on Brookside Lane; my former house was given number 18. I was delighted to see he had saved the trees in front of our house and as many of the others on the property as possible. The land was graded, and the water from the brook diverted through underground pipes to the Rockaway River. With the placement of the eight new homes, I could not determine if my magnificent oak tree survived, but I think it did.

In my last two visits to Montville and Boonton and in writing my reflections on living in these communities, I now have a much different perspective of the area and its history. I can see how the lives of the Van Duyne family, the Adam-Miller family, and those of the Isaac Kingsland family were part of the fabric of early American history. Now when I think of my house in Montville, I can visualize the Van Duynes living there. When I think of my house in Boonton, I can visualize the faces of all those pioneers in the Adam-Miller family and the Isaac Kingsland family who cleared the land and contributed to building the northeastern part of America.

I realize my memories are my treasures, and so I share them with others, much as Alex Fowler did. I cannot control the passing of time. I bless the past for how it nourished and educated me and made me who I am today. But living life deeply means generating new sets of memories and flowing with new experiences and people like a never-ending river. Just as the Rockaway River has traveled through Morris County's history for centuries, life and its memories have no end.

Acknowledgments

Jean Chipman, a previous owner of the Martin J. Van Duyne house, sent me a copy of the Montville Township Historical Society Newsletter. My mother's brother, Uncle Charles Buesing, who once lived in Towaco, had written an article about the Morris Canal in which he mentioned my parents, Bill and Marie Reif.

Prior to receiving the newsletter, I had started writing my early recollections, which covered my life in Montville living in the Martin J. Van Duyne house and later on the Miller-Kingsland property in Boonton. The newsletter and my contact with local historians provided the impetus for including a brief history of the land I lived on in both towns.

Kathy Fisher, president of the Montville Township Historical Society, provided a wealth of information. Among other things, she sent me copies of articles Thelma Van Arsdel wrote for the *Daily Record*. David Phraner, also from the Montville Township Historical Society, became another source of local history. A member of the Canal Society of New Jersey and former member of the Montville Historic Preservation Review Commission, David provided priceless information on the history of the Morris Canal. Walter Doremus Jr. shared his experience regarding the fire that destroyed the Montville Dutch Reformed Church. Evelyn Echardt, a past president of the Boonton Historical Society, was gracious with her time and knowledge in guiding my search of local history.

The source for most of the historical information was *Splinters from the Past: Discovering History in Old Houses*, by Alex D. Fowler. He and Mae Erskine Fowler were our neighbors when we lived in Boonton.

Three other books helped me find particular pieces of history—*The Morris Canal: A Photographic History*, by James Lee; *Boonton Was an Iron Town*, by Peter C. Wendt Jr.; and *Images of America—Montville*, by Patricia Florio Colrick.

Someone who has lived in Morris County for a long time might take its historical treasures for granted. For new residents, a visit to the local historical societies or libraries will open the door to a wealth of history of which they have directly or indirectly become guardians. I have provided a minimal bibliography that will help the adventurous person plot his or her own treasure hunt. The many professionals and volunteers in local historical societies and libraries will assist.

Those readers who do not live in Morris County or who live outside of New Jersey will be exposed to a bit of history of Northern New Jersey and New York City where a good part of our American history started.

When I lived in Montville my parents took me to historical sites in eastern Pennsylvania, Fort Ticonderoga and West Point in New York State, and most of the local historical houses and campgrounds in northern New Jersey. My parents were first generation Americans, who were very interested in early American history and wanted to share it with me. As a young person, I did not fully appreciate the rich history that surrounded me in Montville and Boonton. Now, exploring my roots has become important to me, and, after discovering Alex Fowler's book, I have a more inclusive perspective of the history associated with the land and the families who lived there long before I did. Alexandria Owens, Thelma Van Arsdel's granddaughter, who, with her husband Michael, currently owns the Isaac Harrison Kingsland house, provided current history on the big house.

I also appreciated the assistance of S. Christine Jochem, Department Head of Local History and Genealogy at the Public Library of Morristown and Morris Township, and Claire E. Kissil, librarian in the Local History and Genealogy department of the Joint Free Public Library of Morristown and Morris Township, who helped me with the bibliography selection.

I am very grateful to Lorie Hanna, Pearl Gold, Sue Logston, Elaine Markellos, Estelle Markowich, Paula Reuben, Marcia Cohn Spiegel, and Judy Stock—all dear friends who not only gave me encouragement in my first venture in writing but also urged me to expand my storytelling, all of which added more color and depth to the narrative.

I am deeply indebted to Ed Moulton, my godchild, for first finding me a copy of Alex Fowler's out-of-print book, *Splinters from the Past: Discovering*

History in Old Houses, and then preparing my pictures and the map for publishing.

I am a firm believer that when the student is ready the teacher will appear. That was the case when I attended the 2005 International Women's Writing Guild's summer conference at Skidmore College at Saratoga Springs, New York. Author and journalist Lorraine Ash (*Life Touches Life: A Mother's Story of Stillbirth and Healing*) was conducting the *Writing An Unsinkable Memoir* workshop. Immediately, I felt she was the person to work with me and subsequently she introduced me to Bonnie Nadzeika the director of the Morris County Historical Society and other prominent people in the Morris County historical world.

Notes

Part One: The Martin J. Van Duyne Dutch-American Stone Farmhouse, Montville, New Jersey 1935 to 1944.

1. Alex D. Fowler. *Splinters from the Past: Discovering History in Old Houses.* (Morristown, NJ: Morris County Historical Society, 1984), p. 72.

2. Ibid., p. 73.

3. James Lee. *The Morris Canal, A Photographic History* (Easton, PA: Delaware Press, 1994). A brief history of the Morris Canal supported by pictures taken between Jersey City-Newark and Phillipsburg, NJ. The book is available through the Montville Historical Society among others.

4. Barbara N. Kalata. *A Hundred Years, A Hundred Miles* (Morris County Historical Society, 1983). Limited copies are available from the New Jersey Transportation Heritage Bookshelf, 103 Dogwood Lane, Berkeley Heights, New Jersey.

5. Thelma Van Arsdel. "Montville Church to Mark 200th Anniversary," *Daily Record* (Parsippany, NJ), July 25, 1958.

6. Thelma Van Arsdel. "$40,000 Fire Destroys Old Montville Church," *Daily Record* (Parsippany, NJ), June 28, 1958.

7. Ibid

8. Alex D. Fowler. *Splinters from the Past: Discovering History in Old Houses* (Morristown, NJ: Morris County Historical Society, 1984), 75. Martin J. Van Duyne House, 292 Main Road.

9. Thelma Van Arsdel. "FAI-104 Threatens Pre-Revolutionary Home," *Daily Record* (Parsippany, NJ), August 16, 1958.

Part Two: The Miller-Kingsland Tract, Boonton, New Jersey 1944 to 1954

1. Alex D. Fowler. *Splinters from the Past: Discovering History in Old Houses—Miller-Kingsland House or How I Did It* (Morristown, NJ: Morris County Historical Society, 1984) 177-78.

2. Ibid., p. 171.

3. Peter C. Wendt Jr. *Boonton Was An Iron Town*, (P. Wendt and the Boonton Historical Society, 1976), p. 16.

4. Ibid., p. 11.

5. Ibid., p. 51.

6. Alex D. Fowler. *Splinters from the Past: Discovering History in Old Houses—Miller-Kingsland House or How I Did It*, (Morristown, NJ: Morris County Historical Society, 1984), p. 5.

7. Ibid., p. 2.

8. Peter C. Wendt Jr. *Boonton Was An Iron Town*, (P. Wendt and the Boonton Historical Society, 1976), p. 19.

Bibliography

Colrick, Patricia Florio. *Images of America—Montville*. Charleston, SC: Arcadia Publishing, 2000. A story of Montville through historic pictures of families, houses, and other buildings. Available through the Montville Township Historical Society.

Fowler, Alex D. *Splinters from the Past: Discovering History in Old Houses*. Morristown, NJ: Morris County Historical Society, 1984. A story of historical houses within the Town of Boonton, Boonton Township, Montville Township, Denville Township, Parsippany-Troy Hills, and Mountain Lakes Borough. Currently out of print, but contact the Joint Free Public Library of Morristown and Morris Township.

Kalata, Barbara N. *A Hundred Years, A Hundred Miles*. Morris County Historical Society, 1983. Limited copies are available from the New Jersey Transportation Heritage Bookshelf, 103 Dogwood Lane, Berkeley Heights, New Jersey.

Kimbark, L. S. *A History of Beavertown and Lincoln Park*. rev. ed. Borough of Lincoln Park and the Beavertown Historical Society, 1971. Unfortunately this is out of print.

Lee, James. *The Morris Canal, A Photographic History*. Easton, PA: Delaware Press, 1994. A brief history of the Morris Canal supported by pictures taken between Jersey City-Newark and Phillipsburg, NJ. Available through the Montville Historical Society among others.

Macasek, Joseph J. *Guide to the Morris Canal in Morris County*. Morristown, NJ: Morris County Heritage Commission, 1996. A layman's walking guide to the elusive remains of one of New Jersey's fascinating historic canals. Available through the Montville Historical Society, among others.

Tabor, Thomas T. *Delaware Lackawanna & Western RR, Vols. 1 and 2*. Published by TTT III. (Out of print, but check a local library.)

Wendt, Peter C. Jr. *Boonton Was An Iron Town*. P. Wendt and the Boonton Historical Society, 1976. Available from the Boonton Historical Society.

NOTE: These books are available in the Boonton, Dover, Kinnelon, Lincoln Park, Montville, Morris County, and Pequannock libraries, with the exception of the Kimbark book, which is not available in the Montville Library, as of this writing.

Printed in the United States
74744LV00004B/1-375